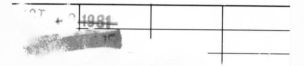

P9-DXH-672

Date Due

1981			

Trees, Shrubs and Flowers of the Midwest

Trees, Shrubs and Flowers of the Midwest

G. Eric Hultman

Illustrations by G. Eric Hultman
and Margaret Hilligoss

Produced by Greatlakes Living Press
of Waukegan, Illinois,
for Contemporary Books, Inc.

cbi Contemporary Books, Inc.
Chicago

Library of Congress Cataloging in Publication Data

Hultman, G. Eric.
   Trees, shrubs, and flowers of the Midwest.

   Includes index.
   1. Botany—Middle West.   2. Plants—Identification.
I. Title.
QK128.H84   1978   582'.0977   78-2897
ISBN 0-8092-7693-3
ISBN 0-8092-7692-5 pbk.

Copyright © 1978 by Greatlakes Living Press
All rights reserved
Published by Contemporary Books, Inc.
180 North Michigan Avenue, Chicago, Illinois 60601
Manufactured in the United States of America
Library of Congress Catalog Card Number: 78-2897
International Standard Book Number: 0-8092-7693-3 (cloth)
                               0-8092-7692-5 (paper)

Published simultaneously in Canada by
Beaverbooks
953 Dillingham Road
Pickering, Ontario L1W 1Z7
Canada

To Nathan Eric: May his generation
find a clean, green world
in which to raise their children.

Note to Reader

This book is not intended to be a thorough treatment
of all plants in the Midwest. Few immigrant species,
for instance, have been included, since most are
considered "weeds." The book reflects my 15 years
as an amateur field naturalist. As I've wandered the
surviving woods, wetlands, and prairies of the Midwest, I have noted the species which I appreciated
most. Although I may have overlooked some rather
outstanding varieties in this text, my intent is to help
you identify plants in their native habitats and to
share the pleasure of growing green things.

Contents

Trees, Shrubs and Flowers of the Midwest

1

Introduction

What is this book?

This book about plants is for people who are curious about the green things that grow around them but who don't have time to become familiar with the biological knowledge so often needed to identify plants.

It is not meant to be a technical tome or a treatise on botany but, rather, a light, hopefully interesting account of plants and the places they dwell. It is meant to find a home with families, campers, fishermen, hunters— all who love the outdoors. People who, for whatever reason, are curious about our green world in central North America.

With this book's clear illustrations and descriptions, as well as some background on the

1

how and why of plant ecology, you can discover for yourself the interesting story plants have to tell!

How this book is organized and why

Plants are found in an almost infinite variety of shapes, colors, and sizes. They are biologically defined by analysis of plant structure, such as number and placement of leaves, type of veining, and number of petals and other flower parts. In addition, a plant's means of reproduction and other physiological factors are also parts of the biological definition. However, most of us don't carry a fund of such knowledge upon which to draw. That's why a technical field guide is of little use to us.

Nothing can dampen your enthusiasm for plant identification more quickly than standing in the still midday heat of a bottomland forest, technical guide in hand, trying to identify the exotic flower your child is accidentally stepping on. While swatting at a cloud of mysterious, tiny, black bugs, you anxiously try to determine whether you are to count the number of petals and divide by three.

So, it is for the nonbotanist that this book is written.

You will find that the book is divided into three main sections: The Prairie, The Woodlands, and The Wetlands. Each of these refers to a very general plant zone that has a some-what distinctive characteristic. Many plant species covered in this book are found in more than one zone but are featured only in the zone where they are most likely to be found.

Each section is broken down into three general groupings: flowers (by color), trees, and shrubs. Habitat information, telling you where the plant is likely to live, can be found throughout.

But be forewarned! Remember that plants have not read the botany texts and field guides and have a tendency to do the unexpected. The proverbial "flower in a crannied nook" will spring up in the most unlikely places at times. Whether an elm seedling in a sidewalk crack or a rugged dandelion rooted in the notch of a tree, some plant seedling is always trying to defy God and science by springing unpredictably forth. A warm December rain will, on rare occasion, cause some early spring plants to blossom, only to be crushed by winter's heel.

This book does not use complex biological terms or description. As such, no plant "keys" have been developed for use, as is often the case with this type of book. Nevertheless, pay close attention to the details of your plant specimen. Does the number of petals match that in the illustration? Is the plant about the right height as given in the plant description?

Are the leaves matched evenly on the stem, or do they alternate from one side to the other? Do the veins on the leaves run parallel or do they branch? Do the leaves have a smooth or a saw-toothed edge? Does the place where you found the plant seem like a logical place for it to grow? Can you find plants that grow in the same habitat? You will have to ask yourself these questions each time you attempt a positive identification. Don't be discouraged. Once you have identified a few plants, it will become much easier.

As you attempt to identify a plant in the midst of the green wilds, be they backyard or bog, ask yourself whether you're in a prairie, woodland, or wetland habitat. Are you looking at a flower, tree, or shrub? Does it seem to be a typical specimen, or are other nearby specimens different? For instance, a willow may be stunted and look like a shrub, while a juniper may appear to be so large that you think of it first as a tree.

Familiarize yourself with the book. Thumb through it on frigid January evenings and try to get your mind off the weather. Keep it in your camper, tackle box, or glove compartment during the summer months so that it's always handy. Above all, use it so that you can experience the special joy of knowing about our green world!

How plants grow and why

Plants are the product of sunlight, ground rocks and minerals (soil), and six billion years of evolution. Green plant life was the pioneer of the earth's primordial seas and, much later, its lands.

Green? Just what is the stuff that makes these things green? It's a substance called chlorophyll, which allowed plants to become "solar powered" long before man ever arrived to worry about alternate energy sources.

The process by which plants use solar energy to make food is called photosynthesis. This involves the absorption of sunlight by the chlorophyll, which, in turn, provides the energy to manufacture carbohydrates from water and carbon dioxide, with life-supporting oxygen as a by-product.

Sounds simple enough, doesn't it? But it is really only the beginning, the beginning of a never-ending cycle. The plant creates oxygen and food for animals. They eat the plant, use its stored energy, and die. The elements of the animal are then returned to the earth, where once again they become food for plants and another photosynthetic process. Of course, this is a simplified version of what happens, but it is the very heartbeat of planet Earth and its ecosystem.

Ecosystem is the name scientists give to this

interaction between living things and the non-living world.

It changes from one place to another. These changes are caused primarily by differences in climate and geography. Take, for example, a desert that is parched by the sun and receives little rain. A complex system of plants is able to exist there because, over a period of thousands of years, the plants have developed mechanisms—such as ways to store water or to stay dormant for long periods of time—that have made it possible for them to make maximum use of occasional moisture. This is called adaptation.

This process has resulted in many specialized plant communities. Plants in the Midwest show adaptation just as desert plants do, though it is less obvious than in the desert.

Habitat is the term used to describe a place where plants grow. The habitats explained in this book are different yet closely related. In the Midwest, prairie, woodland, and wetland habitats are common where the land has not been dominated for other purposes by man. To know these habitats is to know a significant patch of the giant ecosystem called planet Earth.

Where plants grow

The biologic plant zones, or biotic regions, of central North America are fairly distinct, though greatly altered by man since the American Revolution.

This central section of North America (Ontario, Minnesota, Wisconsin, Indiana, Illinois, Iowa, and Missouri) lies at the approximate heart of the continent. The land is generally flat, with gently rolling hills and occasional wide river valleys. Except for a thin strip in the extreme southern portions of Missouri, Indiana, and Illinois, the entire region was repeatedly flattened by mile-high glaciers during the great Ice Age, called the Pleistocene.

The most recent of those glaciers retreated less than 20,000 years ago, or just yesterday, geologically speaking. The effect this event had on the landscape and subsequent plant growth is clearly evident today.

Beginning on the shore of Hudson Bay in northern Ontario, you can find plants that once grew at the foot of the great glaciers. (In fact, some of these same plant species also can be found growing in association with alpine glaciers in the Canadian Rockies.) This brief belt along the frigid shores of the bay is a subarctic tundra dominated by lichens with a spattering of herbaceous plants and stunted trees. As you move southward, the terrain is characterized by stands of low, bushy trees and open, standing, or slow-moving bodies of water. This open forest setting becomes more modified as you continue southward. Eventually, the standing bodies of water become less sterile, supporting a variety of plant life. Some ponds have even become boglike.

Around these ponds you can find dense growths of tamarack, wild cranberry, and sphagnum moss. Farther southward, ranging from southern Ontario into northern Wisconsin and Michigan, rise the tall, dense conifer forests called the North Woods. They are dominated by white and black spruce, balsam fir, larch, and arborvitae.

Two hundred years ago, these forests ranged much farther south, into what is now lower Wisconsin and Michigan. But the great timber drives of the nineteenth century and a few horrendous forest fires destroyed much of them. This destruction made way for marginal farming and the rapid northward spread of the central hardwood forest. Dominated by such trees as maple and oak, it is an ad hoc mixture of hardwood and second-growth conifers that covers much of Wisconsin and Michigan today.

More southward still, you find the remnants of the great central hardwood forest and of the grand prairie.

The hardwood forest was well established in river bottoms, in the unglaciated southern Ozark region and on the East Coast. Portions of eastern Indiana also were dominated by hardwoods.

The once dominant character of the remaining land area was the vast sea of prairie grass known to the first settlers of the region. They were primarily Frenchmen, who, upon first witnessing the awesome expanse of tall plants, could find only one word in their language to describe it: *prairie,* meaning meadow.

As the great forest of the north fell before the axe, so the grand prairie, or great meadow, fell before the steel plow. Up until the advent of this technological breakthrough, the prairie was considered useless wasteland because the root masses of the prairie plants were so thick that no known method of cultivation would work. Even with a steel plow, a plot of virgin prairie being plowed for the first time might require the brawn of five oxen to cut a straight furrow.

Throughout the glaciated region there remain the characteristic bodies of water described earlier. These glacial "puddles" become fewer as one travels south. Many of these wetlands have followed the course of their natural evolution from clear, sterile lake to vibrant, life-filled lagoons or ponds, and then as they become shallower, to a bog or marsh, and finally to a prairie meadow. But many more wetlands never were able to finish their evolution. Thousands upon thousands of wetland acres were ditched and drained to create more land for the plow.

As a consequence of all this action upon the land, many plant species that once were common are now far less so. In fact, some plant species are now endangered and protected by state or federal laws.

This book deals with common native plants still found in these various plant communities. Of course, the grand prairie is all but gone, surviving in only a few protected sanctuaries and old cemeteries. But many of the plant species that once made up the biotic zones of pre-Revolutionary America are still around. Their diversity and adaptability have withstood the march of "progress."

Prairie plants find root in fallow fields, roadsides, and other open lands. Timber-rich river bottoms can still be found providing a canopy and shelter to dozens of woodland plant species. And many wetland species, among the most diverse and adaptable, continue to defy "progress" by sprouting in the very ditches designed to destroy their home!

2

The Prairie

For our generation to know the vastness and beauty that once was the grand prairie is an impossibility. In its place has grown the patchwork quilt that is the fields of the world's richest agricultural land. Now it is difficult to imagine hundreds of miles of uninterrupted flatlands stretching to an infinite horizon; a jungle of big bluestem and golden sunflowers reaping sunshine and untamed wind. Nothing dominated this environment. The native American and the bison learned to abide with it, not master it. Even forests to the north, east, and south submitted to its will.

A combination of environmental factors led to this great prairie, the benefits of which we still reap from its ancient humus. Moisture and sunshine played their part, but similar amounts of both were present elsewhere on the continent without resultant prairie development. It wasn't weather that fostered the prairie, but fire! High winds, made more intense by flatland, as well as the repetitive cycle of summer drought made for hot, fast-moving fires. All but the toughest sapling could find itself blisteringly girdled in a matter of seconds with no hope for survival. Only a handful of oak groves managed to establish themselves in the prairie region, protected by a phalanx of bristly bur oaks. These groves later became "islands" for migrating settlers. Many places in the Midwest prairie region still reflect this past with such names as Kennicot Grove and Funk's Grove.

If the fire was severe enough to stop the advancing forest, why didn't it kill the grass? Well, although the fire could heat the top half-inch of soil to about 400 degrees in a minute or two, the soil below was just barely affected, protecting the life-giving roots of the grass.

The roots of the plants in a prairie community are well developed, often 15 to 20 feet long. These long roots allow the plants to draw on groundwater in time of drought.

Prairie plants are relatively long-lived perennials. The upper parts die back to ground level every autumn, but the roots remain alive. Because of the severe competition for water, light, and the nutrients that occurred in the dense virgin prairie, it was essential for these plants to maintain themselves from year to year rather than starting from seed each growing season.

More than 45 different plant families are found in the prairie plant community. Many are represented by only one or two species; others, a half-dozen or more. For instance, the sunflower family is characterized by bright flowers that grow among tall grasses from spring to fall. The pea family is also a populous midwestern prairie species. Collectively, the brilliant flowers of the prairie are referred to as "forbs" by the botanists.

However, grasses dominated the prairie throughout its range, from its eastern limits in Indiana and southern Michigan, westward to the Rockies. The midwestern prairie region received more rain than the western section. The result was a thicker, taller prairie, the tallgrass prairie.

In the tallgrass region an average of about 35 inches of rain fell annually. This dense, high prairie could quite frequently engulf a man on horseback. One could ride through the prairie and not see the horizon.

Of course, the prairie varied widely from one area to the next. Soil types and their varying ability to hold moisture exerted a great influence on the type and extent of prairie plants. About five general types of prairie are recognized today: medium-moist (mesic) prairies; high, dry prairies; low prairies; prairie marshes; and alkaline (fen) prairies.

Although the prairie as we once knew it is all but gone, its biological legacy lives on in the hundreds of diverse plant species that survive wherever open ground and sunlight come together to form the right conditions for growth.

Remember, some plants that perhaps were once common have all but disappeared. In this book you will find a selection of prairie plants you are likely to find today in any open, sunny spot lying fallow, or undisturbed.

Try to find a patch of relatively undisturbed land in an old cemetery, churchyard, state park, or preserve. Perhaps you may discover a prairie remnant near your home that is worth having an expert examine. Many patches of the original prairie still remain but are usually less than an acre in size.

When the last weeks in August come to the land that once was the grand prairie, watch for the tallest forbs. Their varied, bright yellow heads form dense, high crests on roadsides and fields, a dazzling reminder that once upon a time they stretched in an unbroken field of dancing gold, straight to a blue-sky horizon.

Flowers

Culver's Root

Culver's Root
WHITE
(*Veronicastrum virginicum*)

This member of the snapdragon family favors
meadows and moist prairie thickets. Three to
7 slender, sharp-toothed leaves radiate from
the stalk. Flowers bloom in tapering, dense
clusters June through September.

HEIGHT: 2 to 7 feet.
RANGE: Illinois, Wisconsin, Ontario.

Rattlesnake Master

Rattlesnake Master   WHITE
(*Eryngium yuccifolium*)

This member of the parsley family is found in prairies, thickets, and open woods. It is a major component of the tallgrass prairie. Yuccalike leaves are spiny edged, leathery, and up to 3 feet long. They are attached to a tough, coarse stalk. Flowers are roundheaded, with tiny, 5-parted sections that are often hidden by hoodlike modified leaves. Blooms September to November.

HEIGHT: 3 to 4 feet.
RANGE: Throughout Midwest except Ontario.

Rock Jasmine

Rock Jasmine

WHITE

(Androsace occidentalis)

This very small member of the primrose family is an annual, an unusual type for the dense prairie, where conditions favor the perennial flower. The plant can be distinguished by the numerous half-inch leaves that radiate from the base of the stem. Small flowers on short, radiating stems that look like an inverted umbrella. Blooms April to June.

HEIGHT: 3 inches.
RANGE: Common in Illinois, Wisconsin.

Canada Windflower

Canada Windflower   WHITE
(Anemone canadensis)

This habitant of meadows and wet prairie has
no petals but instead has sepals that look like
petals. The leaf is composed of 3 stalkless
leaflets. Blooms May through July.

HEIGHT: 1 foot.
RANGE: Illinois, Missouri.

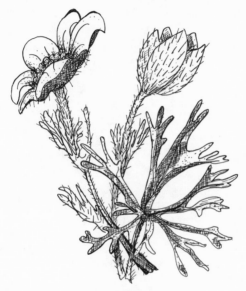

Pasqueflower

Pasqueflower   WHITE/BLUE VIOLET
(Anemone patens)

This plant grows from an underground stem.
It is covered with silky hairs and has a deeply
toothed leaf. Five to 7 petallike sepals bloom
in March and April and appear before the
leaves.

HEIGHT: 16 inches.
RANGE: Illinois, Iowa, Minnesota, Wisconsin,
          Missouri, Michigan.

Stiff Sandwort

Stiff Sandwort   WHITE
(*Arenaria stricta*)

High, dry prairie and rocky soil are preferred
by this plant. It is dense with many branches.
Needlelike leaves grow with tufts of shorter
leaves at the junction of the leaf stem and
stalk. The flower has 5 rounded petals that are
slightly notched. Blooms June through July.

HEIGHT: 6 to 12 inches.
RANGE: Illinois.

White False Indigo

White False Indigo

WHITE

(Baptisia leucantha)

This plant is found in low prairies and open woodland. It is bushy and many branched, with thick stems. Leaves are divided into 3 sections and are broader toward the tips, with a short leafstalk. The leaves turn black when dried. The flower has 5 lobes, 2 upper and 3 lower. Blooms June through August.

HEIGHT: 6 feet.
RANGE: Illinois, Minnesota, Ontario, Wisconsin.

Indian Plantain

Indian Plantain   WHITE
(Cacalia tuberosa)

Low prairies and marshes are the habitat of
this plant. Large, coarse, thick leaves are oval
shaped and pointed, with smooth edges. A
flat-topped flower cluster blooms June through
August.

HEIGHT: 2 to 6 feet.
RANGE: Illinois, Minnesota, Ontario, Indiana,
         Wisconsin.

Upright Bindweed

Upright Bindweed
(Convolvulus spithamaeus)

WHITE/PINK

This downy, twining plant of dry prairie often disappears from mature prairie land. Leaves have pointed lobes at the base and are oval shaped. The flower is funnel shaped and about 2 inches long. Blooms May through July.

HEIGHT: Up to 2 feet.
RANGE: Illinois, Iowa, Missouri, Minnesota, Ontario.

Shooting Star

Shooting Star   WHITE/LAVENDER
(Dodecatheon meadia)

This member of the primrose family favors
damp prairie, meadows, and open woods. Oblong leaves—3 to 12 inches long, lance shaped,
and smooth—radiate from the base of a leafless stem. Petals are swept back, and a pointed
beaklike structure points downward from the
mouth of the flower, which blooms in May.

HEIGHT: 1 foot.
RANGE: Illinois, Indiana, Iowa, Wisconsin.

Common Strawberry

Common Strawberry   WHITE
(*Fragaria virginiana*)

This short, bushy, hairy plant is found in fields
and open places. Leaves consist of 3 sharp-
toothed segments on long stems and grow
from short underground stalks. The flower has
5 rounded petals. The delectable fruit is red
and has small seeds embedded in the center.
The plant is an extremely variable species and
the basic stock from which hybrids were
developed for cultivation.

HEIGHT: 3 to 6 inches
RANGE: Throughout Midwest.

Northern Bedstraw

Northern Bedstraw   WHITE
(Galium boreale)

This plant occurs in damp prairie. Narrow, lance-shaped leaves radiate in sets of 4 from a smooth, square stalk. Four-petaled, tiny flowers bloom in multiple clusters May through August.

HEIGHT: 12 to 30 inches.
RANGE: Illinois, Indiana, Michigan, Missouri.

Prairie White-fringed Orchis

Prairie White-fringed Orchis   <small>WHITE</small>
(Habenaria leucophaea)

This fragrant plant of wet prairies and sphagnum bogs has lance-shaped leaves that are 4 to 8 inches long. A 3-lipped, fringed flower blooms on a spike June through July.

HEIGHT: 1 to 3 feet.
RANGE: Great Lakes area.

Roundheaded Bush Clover

Roundheaded Bush Clover   WHITE
(Lespedeza capitata)

This plant is found in dry, sandy soil of fields and prairie. It is a bushy, variable plant, with a silvery green color caused by flat-lying silky hairs. Leaves are made up of 3 narrow leaflets arranged in threes like a true clover. Flowers are dense, bristly clusters of small, pealike flowers. Blooms August through September.

HEIGHT: 2 to 5 feet.
RANGE: Illinois, Wisconsin, Minnesota.

Pale Spiked Lobelia

Pale Spiked Lobelia
(Lobelia spicata)

WHITE/BLUE

This prairie plant has small, lance-shaped leaves that are nearly toothless and connected directly to the stalk. The small flower has 2 narrow lobes above and 3 lobes forming a lip below and blooms on a spike on the upper part of the stem June through August.

HEIGHT: 15 inches.
RANGE: Throughout Midwest.

Cowbane

Cowbane
WHITE

(Oxypolis rigidior)

This plant is found in wet prairie and swamps. The leaflets are toothed, 6 inches long, and either sharp pointed or very narrow without teeth. Umbrellalike clusters of flowers bloom August through September. Juices are poisonous.

HEIGHT: 2 to 6 feet.
RANGE: Upper Midwest.

Wild Quinine

Wild Quinine   WHITE
(*Parthenium integrifolium*)

Dry prairies and bluffs are the habitat of this plant. Large leaves at the base are toothed, rough, and long stalked. Leaves attached to the stem may have no stalk. Five differentiated flowers grow on each cluster; other flowers are small and numerous. Blooms June through September.

HEIGHT: 1½ to 3 feet.
RANGE: Upper Midwest except Ontario.

Pale Beard Tongue

Pale Beard Tongue   WHITE
(Penstemon pallidus)

This is a plant of high, dry prairie and fields. Stalkless leaves occur in pairs on the stem and occasionally have teeth. The tubular, 5-lobed flower has a white blossom with pink lines inside. Blooms April to June.

HEIGHT: 3 feet.
RANGE: Illinois, Indiana, Michigan, Iowa, Missouri.

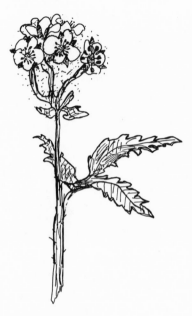

Prairie Cinquefoil

Prairie Cinquefoil WHITE
(Potentilla arguta)

This member of the rose family is found in rocky soils of prairie and dry woods. Seven to 11 oval-shaped leaflets are downy underneath and attached to a coarse, hairy stem. Numerous 5-petaled flowers bloom June through August.

HEIGHT: 1 to 3 feet.
RANGE: Illinois, Indiana, Missouri.

Swamp Saxifrage

Swamp Saxifrage   WHITE/GREEN/YELLOW
(Saxifraga pennsylvanica)   /PURPLE

This plant is common to wet prairie, as well as swamp and bog. It is found in at least 4 color varieties. Blunt, lance-shaped, toothless leaves, 4 to 10 inches long, sometimes have shallow teeth. A 5-petaled flower blooms May through June and can be white, green, yellow, purple, or something in between.

HEIGHT: 20 to 48 inches.
RANGE: Illinois, Missouri, Wisconsin, Minnesota, Ontario.

Starry False Solomon's Seal

Starry False Solomon's Seal   WHITE
(Smilacina stellata)

This member of the lily family prefers prairie; moist, open ground; and sand dunes. Broad leaves with parallel veins clasp a zigzag stem at their base. Tiny flowers bloom at the stem tip May through July. Later a brownish or speckled berry is produced, which turns red or black when fully ripened.

HEIGHT: 1 foot.
RANGE: Illinois, Missouri.

Purple Meadow Rue

Purple Meadow Rue
(Thalictrum dasycarpum)

WHITE

This tall member of the buttercup family is found in meadows and wet prairie thickets. Leaves are divided into 3 segments, which in turn are divided into threes. Undersides of the leaf are downy. Clusters of fuzzy, white flowers tinged with brown or purple bloom from a purple stem May through July.

HEIGHT: 2 to 6 feet.
RANGE: Throughout Midwest.

White Clover

White Clover   WHITE/PINK
(Trifolium repens)

This prairie clover has a creeping stem. Leaves
are fairly typical of clover—divided into 3
leaflets on long stalks. Each leaflet is marked
with a pale green triangle. Flowers bloom in
dense clusters in globular heads on leafless
stalks May through October.

HEIGHT: 4 to 10 inches.
RANGE: Throughout Midwest.

Edible Valerian

Edible Valerian   WHITE/PINK
(*Valeriana ciliata*)

This plant is found in wet, open places like meadows. Thick leaves have parallel veins and are arranged in pairs. Many small flowers bloom at stem tips and branches in May.

HEIGHT: 20 inches.
RANGE: Illinois, Iowa, Minnesota, Ontario.

Prairie Coreopsis

Prairie Coreopsis
(Coreopsis palmata)

YELLOW

This plant is found in prairie and open woods. Leaves are smooth, rigid, and crow's-foot shaped, with 3 lobes. A showy, daisylike flower blooms June through July.

HEIGHT: 1 to 3 feet.

RANGE: Illinois, Indiana, Wisconsin, Missouri, Michigan.

Sneezeweed

Sneezeweed   YELLOW
(Helenium autumnale)

Dense prairie, wet meadows, and swampy
areas are the preferred habitat of this daisylike
flower. Sometimes called false sunflower, it is
distinguished by a yellow button, or center, in
the flower head. Swept-back, petallike rays
have 3 scallops at each tip. Leaves are narrow,
undivided, lance shaped, and sometimes
toothed. They are attached to the stalk singly
and are 2 to 4 inches long. Blooms August
through October.

HEIGHT: 2 to 5 feet.
RANGE: Illinois, Wisconsin, Minnesota, Iowa.

Saw-toothed Sunflower

Saw-toothed Sunflower
(Helianthus grosseserratus)

YELLOW

Very similar to the common sunflower, it is found along roadsides and in most prairies. Leaves are saw-toothed on the edge, lance shaped and arranged in pairs on the stalk. Blooms July through October.

HEIGHT: 4 to 10 feet.
RANGE: Illinois, Minnesota.

Oxeye

Oxeye   YELLOW
(Heliopsis helianthoides)

Sometimes called false sunflower, this plant is not a true sunflower. It has petallike rays and a conical center. Oval-to-lance-shaped leaves can be either smooth or rough. They are attached in pairs to a smooth stem. Blooms July to September.

HEIGHT: 5 feet.
RANGE: Illinois, Ontario, Wisconsin, Minnesota.

Yellow Star Grass

Yellow Star Grass   YELLOW
(Hypoxis hirsuta)

This member of the daffodil family has hairy,
grasslike, shiny, and narrow leaves. Six-
pointed, starlike flowers with 2 to 7 blooms on
a slender stem in May.

HEIGHT: 4 to 6 inches.
RANGE: Illinois, Wisconsin.

Two-eyed Cynthia

Two-eyed Cynthia   YELLOW/ORANGE
(*Krigia biflora*)

Because its highly variable leaves can look
very much like a dandelion's, this plant is also
called false dandelion. Leaves are toothed or
lobed and grow from the base of the stem.
The stem may have a few leaves, and the
flower has numerous petallike rays. Blooms
May to August.

HEIGHT: 2 feet.
RANGE: Illinois, Indiana, Missouri.

Prairie Loosestrife

Prairie Loosestrife
YELLOW

(Lysimachia quadriflora)

This member of the primrose family prefers wetter prairie soil. Leaves are very narrow and stiff, almost needlelike, and usually arranged in pairs on the stalk. Five-petaled flowers are slightly toothed at the edge and bloom July through August.

HEIGHT: 1 to 3 feet.

RANGE: Throughout Midwest.

Prairie Coneflower

Prairie Coneflower   YELLOW
(*Ratibida pinnata*)

The leaves of this plant of prairies and dry woods are deeply pointed and consist of 3 to 7 segments that are often toothed and hairy. A flower with petallike rays that are swept back from a gray button, or center, blooms June through August.

HEIGHT: 4 feet.
RANGE: Throughout Midwest.

Black-eyed Susan

Black-eyed Susan　　　　　YELLOW/ORANGE
(Rudbeckia hirta)

A member of the daisy family that favors dry fields, prairies, and roadsides, this plant is usually not found on mature or climax prairie. It is generally a biannual flower, but some plants occasionally bloom every year. Leaves and stem are bristly with hairs. Leaves are undivided, usually with a toothed edge. They are oval shaped near the base of the stem, narrower and more linear near the top. A single flower head, with 10 to 20 petallike rays and a dark brown center that is cone shaped or domed, blooms June through October.

HEIGHT:　1 to 3 feet.
RANGE:　Throughout Midwest.

Rosinweed

Rosinweed   YELLOW
(Silphium integrifolium)

Resembling sunflowers, this plant prefers
roadsides, prairies, and open woods. Large,
rough, oval-shaped leaves may or may not
have teeth. They are paired and attached
directly to the stem, which has a thick, resinous juice. The flower has several petallike rays
and blooms July through September.

HEIGHT: 2 to 6 feet.
RANGE: Illinois, Missouri, Minnesota, Wis-
          consin, Iowa.

Prairie Dock

Prairie Dock
(Silphium terebinthinaceum)

YELLOW

A conspicuous prairie flower, this thick-stemmed giant is similar to a sunflower. It is distinguished by the huge, slightly heart-shaped leaves that grow on the first 2 feet of the stem. Numerous petallike rays character-ize the flower head, which blooms August through October.

HEIGHT: 4 to 10 feet.
RANGE: Illinois, Minnesota, Ontario, Missouri.

Late Goldenrod

Late Goldenrod
YELLOW

(Solidago gigantea)

This plant, largest of the goldenrods, is an inhabitant of moist, open thickets. Leaves have parallel veins and are sharply toothed. A branched, plumelike flower mass gently curves from the top of the pale green or purplish stem. Hundreds of fuzzy, tiny blossoms grace the plume. Blooms August through October.

HEIGHT: 2 to 7 feet.
RANGE: Throughout Midwest.

Showy Goldenrod

Showy Goldenrod   YELLOW
(Solidago speciosa)

Of the 75 species of goldenrod that are found in the northeastern United States, this is perhaps the most beautiful. It is found in prairie thickets and fields. Leaves have no teeth but rather irregular edges. The stem is stout, smooth, and slightly reddish. A long, dense, almost cylindrical plume of large fuzzy flower heads blooms August to October.

HEIGHT: 2 to 6 feet.
RANGE: Upper Midwest.

Golden Alexander

Golden Alexander   YELLOW
(Zizia aurea)

This member of the parsley family grows in meadows and wet thickets. Leaves are in 3 sections, each divided into 3 to 7 narrow, toothed leaflets. The stem is often tinged red. Flower clusters bloom in May.

HEIGHT: 20 inches.
RANGE: Throughout Midwest.

Butterfly Weed

Butterfly Weed   ORANGE
(Asclepias tuberosa)

Although a member of the milkweed family, it does not have the thick, milky juice in its leaves and stems as other milkweeds do. It prefers dry, open land and roadsides. Leaves grow singly, and stalks are hairy. Flowers have petals bent back sharply and support 5 cups with 5 incurved "horns." Blooms June through September.

HEIGHT: 1 to 2 feet.
RANGE: Illinois, Missouri, Minnesota, Ontario

Michigan Lily

Michigan Lily   ORANGE
(Lilium michiganese)

This pretty flower with its spotted blossoms is found in prairie meadows and open woods. Blooms June through July.

HEIGHT: 4 feet.
RANGE: Throughout Midwest.

Hoary Puccoon

Hoary Puccoon   ORANGE/YELLOW
(*Lithospermum canescens*)

These colorful spring plants, found in dry or sandy soils, are covered with a dense, white down. Leaves are toothless and slender and are 2 to 20 inches long. Flowers bloom in flat or bent-over clusters May through June.

HEIGHT: 8 to 12 inches.
RANGE: Illinois, Wisconsin, Ontario, Indiana, Michigan.

Nodding Wild Onion

Nodding Wild Onion   PINK/RED
(Allium cernuum)

This narrow-leaved member of the lily family grows in open woodlands, as well as prairie. It is similar to the wild onion of very low prairies. A crook at the top of the stem causes the pretty clusters of flowers to hang over. Blooms in July and August.

HEIGHT: 1 to 2 feet.
RANGE: Illinois, Michigan, Minnesota.

Spreading Dogbane

Spreading Dogbane
(Apocynum androsaemifolium)

PALE PINK

This fragrant, shrublike flower often bordered oak thickets on the old prairie and still does in some places. Oval-shaped leaves are set in pairs on the ruddy stem, which forks repeatedly, giving an appearance of no main stem, and yields a milky juice when broken. Clusters of nodding, bell-shaped flowers hang from the ends of hooked stalks. Interior of flower is striped with deep rose. Blooms June through July. Pioneers used the tough stem fibers as a substitute for hemp.

HEIGHT: 1 to 4 feet.
RANGE: Common in Illinois, Missouri.

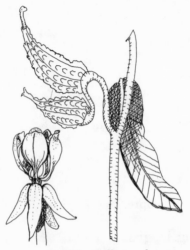

Prairie Milkweed

Prairie Milkweed   PINK/RED/PURPLE
(Asclepias sullivantii)

A milkweed, it oozes a thick, milky white juice if broken. It favors damp ground and open places. Smooth, blunt leaves grow paired or radiate from the stalk, to which they are attached directly. Each flower of the domed, umbrellalike cluster has sharply bent-back petals that support 5 cups with 5 incurved "horns." Blooms June through July.

HEIGHT: 5 feet.
RANGE: Missouri, Minnesota, Ontario.

Indian Paintbrush

Indian Paintbrush   RED
(*Castilleja coccinea*)

This colorful member of the snapdragon family is found in meadows and prairies. It has 3-lobed, scarlet-tipped modified leaves that are attached singly. They almost hide the green-to-yellow flowers, which bloom in a thick spike May through July.

HEIGHT: 1 to 2 feet.
RANGE: Wisconsin, Michigan, Ontario.

Showy Tick Trefoil

Showy Tick Trefoil   PINK
(*Desmodium canadense*)

This bushy member of the pea family is cloverlike, with 3 long, oval leaflets, set in threes.
Half-inch, pealike blossoms are clustered at
the top of a hairy leaf stem. Blooms July
through August.

HEIGHT: 2 to 6 feet.
RANGE: Illinois, Wisconsin, Missouri.

Purple Coneflower

Purple Coneflower
(Echinacea purpurea)

RED/PURPLE

An inhabitant of prairies and dry clearings, this daisylike plant is one of several similar species of prairie plants. Lance-shaped leaves with rough teeth are longer near the base of the plant. Petallike rays radiating from the button, or center, are swept back and often toothed at the outside edge. The solitary flower blooms June through October.

HEIGHT: 2 to 3 feet.
RANGE: Illinois, Michigan, Iowa.

Fireweed

Fireweed
ROSE/PINK
(Epilobium angustifolium)

This remarkable plant can survive extremes of heat and cold. It is the first plant to reappear after a prairie or forest fire. It has willowlike, lance-shaped leaves on alternate sides of the stem. The drooping flower has 4 roundish petals that bloom July through September. Ripened seedpods angle upward on a slender spike, and the seeds have a tuft of hair at one end.

HEIGHT: 3 to 7 feet.
RANGE: Indiana, Missouri, Iowa, Wisconsin, Michigan, Minnesota.

Spotted Joe-Pye Weed

Spotted Joe-Pye Weed   PINK/PURPLE
(*Eupatorium maculatum*)

A common inhabitant of prairie meadows, it is one of 4 species that are similar and commonly called joe-pye weed. Leaves radiate in sets of 4 or 5 from the stalk and have the fragrance of vanilla extract when crushed. Fuzzy, massive, domed, or flat-topped clusters of flowers attached to a purple or purple-spotted stem bloom July through September.

HEIGHT: 2 to 7 feet.
RANGE: Illinois, Indiana, Wisconsin.

Long Plumed Purple Avens

Long Plumed Purple Avens   RED/PURPLE
(Geum triflorum)

This plant of high, dry prairie is characterized by very long, feathery hairs that protrude from the seedpod, looking like an inverted feather duster. Lower leaves are divided into paired, irregular segments with jagged edges. Flowers usually bloom in threes April through June.

HEIGHT: 6 to 16 inches.
RANGE: Great Lakes area.

Rough Blazing Star

Rough Blazing Star   PINK/RED
(*Liatris aspera*)

A highly variable species, this plant can be
difficult to identify. Generally, it prefers dry,
sandy soil in open prairie. The single narrow,
lance-shaped leaf is rough. Its crowded flower
spike, which grows on a stalk, contains 25 to
40 florets and blooms August to September.

HEIGHT: 6 to 30 inches.
RANGE: Illinois, Indiana, Wisconsin, Ontario.

Winged Loosestrife

Winged Loosestrife
(Lythrum alatum)

PINK/PURPLE

This plant is an inhabitant of wetter prairies. Leaves are oval shaped, with the lower ones set in pairs on the branching, squarish stem and the upper leaves found singly. Six-petaled flowers bloom in spikes June through September.

HEIGHT: 1 to 4 feet.
RANGE: Upper Midwest.

Wild Bergamot

Wild Bergamot
(*Monarda fistulosa*)

PINK/WHITE

A member of the mint family, it has the characteristic mint aroma. Toothed, pointed leaves are set in pairs on a squarish stalk. The flower is tubelike, with a long, narrow curve ending in a ragged "pompom." The lower lip hangs sharply downward. Blooms July through August.

HEIGHT: 5 feet.
RANGE: Illinois, Wisconsin, Minnesota.

Lousewort

Lousewort
RED/YELLOW
(Pedicularis canadensis)

This spring flower of wet meadows is a hairy plant with reddish, deeply toothed, and pointed leaves. The flower is tube shaped; a 2-sectioned upper lip hangs in a hoodlike manner over the mouth of the flower, and the lower lip has 3 spreading lobes. Blooms April to June.

HEIGHT: 5 to 14 inches.
RANGE: Wisconsin, Illinois.

Purple Prairie Clover

Purple Prairie Clover   ROSE/PURPLE
(Petalostemum purpureum)

Dry, sandy prairie is preferred by this plant.
Pointed leaves divide into 3 to 5 hairlike
segments. Flowers are dense spikes on thin
wiry stems. It is a nutritious forage for livestock. Blooms July to August.

HEIGHT: 2 to 3 feet.
RANGE: Illinois, Missouri.

False Dragonhead

False Dragonhead   PINK/RED
(Physostegia virginiana)

This member of the mint family looks like a snapdragon. It favors wetter prairie and thickets, as well as riverbanks. Small, narrow, sharply toothed leaves are attached to a squarish stem. Flowers bloom in a simple spike at the top of a stem June through September.

HEIGHT: 1 to 4 feet.
RANGE: Illinois, Wisconsin, Minnesota, Missouri.

Purple Milkwort

Purple Milkwort
(Polygala polygama)

PINK/ROSE

This plant has leaves that are attached singly to the stem. Numerous short, cloverlike flowers with 3 petals bloom June through July.

HEIGHT: 4 to 12 inches.
RANGE: Upper Midwest.

Field Milkwort

Field Milkwort

ROSE/WHITE

(*Polygala sanguinea*)

This plant favors fields and meadows. Linear, narrow leaves are attached singly and alternately to the stem. A 3-petaled flower with many parts creates the clover look.

HEIGHT: 5 to 15 inches.
RANGE: Minnesota, Ontario.

Meadow Rose

Meadow Rose

PINK

(Rosa carolina)

This pretty, wild rose favors rocky fields and grazed prairie. It has thin, straight thorns. Five to 7 leaflets, slightly toothed at the margins, make up the leaf. Five-petaled flowers bloom June through July.

HEIGHT: 1 to 3 feet.
RANGE: Upper Midwest.

Rough Hedge Nettle

Rough Hedge Nettle   PINK/RED
(Stachys tenuifolia)

This member of the mint family inhabits meadows and wet roadsides. A bristly, square stem with lance-shaped, pointed leaves is topped by a terminal cluster of hooded flowers. Blooms July through September.

HEIGHT: 1 to 5 feet.
RANGE: Upper Midwest.

Western Ironweed

Western Ironweed   PINK
(*Vernonia fasciculata*)

This very bushy plant is common to both
prairie and bottomland. A dense flower mass
in a flat cluster tops off a thick, branching
stem of numerous smooth leaves. Blooms July
through September.

HEIGHT: 2 to 6 feet.
RANGE: Throughout Midwest.

Blue Vervain

Blue Vervain   BLUE
(*Verbena hastata*)

This plant prefers prairie thickets and roadsides. Leaves are narrow, with saw-toothed
edges, and may have 3 lobes. They are attached by leafstalks to a grooved, squarish
stem. Branching, pencillike spikes of 5-petaled
flowers bloom a few at a time from July
through September.

HEIGHT: 5 feet.
RANGE: Throughout Midwest.

Wild Lupine

Wild Lupine

BLUE

(Lupinus perennis)

This member of the pea family favors dry soil of clearings and open woods. It is the only lupine native to the eastern United States. Leaves are made up of 7 to 9 segments arranged palmlike at the top of a long stalk. Flowers have an upper and a lower lip. Blooms May through July.

HEIGHT: 1 to 2 feet.
RANGE: Throughout Midwest.

Wild Hyacinth

Wild Hyacinth   BLUE
(Camassia scilloides)

Meadows, open woods, and roadsides are preferred by this plant. Leaves are 5 to 15 inches
long. Six-pointed, star-shaped flowers on separate stalks bloom May through June.

HEIGHT: 1 to 2 feet.
RANGE: Illinois, Iowa, Minnesota, Michigan,
           Ontario, Wisconsin.

Fringed Gentian

Fringed Gentian
BLUE
(Gentiana crinita)

This pretty flower of wet sand prairies and bogs has smooth-edged, broad, oval leaves set in pairs on the stem. The flower has 4 delicately fringed petals flaring out from a deep tube. Blooms July through October.

HEIGHT: 6 to 20 inches.
RANGE: Illinois, Indiana, Iowa, Ohio, Wisconsin, Ontario.

Prairie Gentian

Prairie Gentian   BLUE
(*Gentiana puberula*)

This plant prefers prairie and open woods
with dry, sandy soil. The pretty, vaselike
flower has 5 points with no fringes and blooms
in a tight cluster September through October.

HEIGHT: 8 to 20 inches.
RANGE: Illinois, Wisconsin, Michigan, Min-
          nesota, Ontario.

Purple False Foxglove

Purple False Foxglove   PURPLE
(Gerardia purpurea)

This member of the snapdragon family prefers
damp, acid soil. Straight, linear leaves are set
in pairs on the stalk. Bell-like flowers with
very short stems bloom from the joint of leaf
and stalk August to September.

HEIGHT: 1 to 3 feet.
RANGE: Illinois, Indiana, Michigan, Minnesota, Wisconsin.

Leadplant

Leadplant   VIOLET/BLUE
(Amorpha canescens)

This is a pealike plant with grayish green foliage covered with white hairs. One-fourth-inch-long, deeply pointed leaflets growing in opposing rows with 15 to 50 in each leaf. The 1-petaled flower blooms in a 2-inch-long spike June through August. The short seedpod has only 1 or 2 seeds.

HEIGHT: 2 to 3 feet.
RANGE: Illinois, Indiana, Missouri, Wisconsin, Michigan.

Small Skullcap

Small Skullcap
VIOLET/BLUE
(Scutellaria parvula)

This member of the mint family has creeping
stems with strings of small tubes. The hairy
leaf has 2 or 3 scallops on its edge and is less
than 1 inch long. Leaves are arranged in pairs
on the stalk and are directly attached. Hoodlike flowers bloom singly from the junction of
leaf and stem May through July.

HEIGHT: 3 to 12 inches.
RANGE: Illinois, Wisconsin, Minnesota.

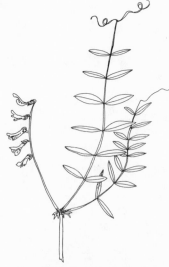

American Vetch

American Vetch
(*Vicia americana*)

PURPLE/VIOLET

This member of the pea family grows in prairies and meadows but generally disappears from both when they reach maturity. The smooth, vinelike plant climbs by tendrils. Leaves have 4 to 8 paired leaflets, usually tipped with a small point. A loose arrangement of 3 to 9 flowers blooms at the junction of leaf with stem May through July.

HEIGHT: 2 to 3 feet.
RANGE: Illinois, Indiana.

Bird's-foot Violet

Bird's-foot Violet
(Viola pedata)

VIOLET

This plant grows in dry, sandy fields or among rocks that receive a great deal of sun. Leaves are finely segmented with 9 to 15 separations and, with a little imagination, look like bird claws. They stay green through winter. The 5-petaled, pansy-shaped flower is sometimes bi-colored, with bottom petal pointed sharply into a sac or spur. Blooms April through June.

HEIGHT: 4 to 10 inches.
RANGE: Throughout Midwest.

Bastard Toadflax

Bastard Toadflax   GREENISH WHITE
(Comandra umbellata)

This unusual plant actually is a small parasitic
species that grows on the roots of other plants.
It prefers dry soil and cover. Leaves are attached singly, and a cluster of greenish white
flowers blooms April to June at the top of the
stem.

HEIGHT: 8 inches.
RANGE: Indiana, Michigan.

Prairie Alumroot

Prairie Alumroot   GREEN WITH RED
(Heuchera richardsonii)

This subdued plant of prairies and dry woods
has leaves shaped like those of a maple tree.
Highly symmetrical flowers are bell shaped,
hanging from short, branching stems. Blooms
April to June.

HEIGHT: 2 to 3 feet.
RANGE: Illinois, Indiana, Michigan, Wiscon-
          sin, Minnesota.

Grasses

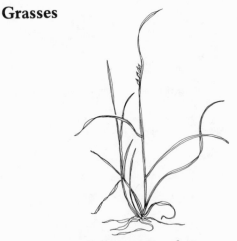

Common Quack Grass

Common Quack Grass
(*Agropyron repens*)

This wheatlike member of the barley tribe is a sod-forming grass. Leaves ⅜ of an inch wide grow in stiff, erect spikes. A set of 3 to 7 flowers with short bristles bloom clustered in a spikelet June through August.

HEIGHT: 3 feet.

RANGE: Common throughout Midwest except Ontario.

Big Bluestem

Big Bluestem
(Andropogon gerardi)

A monarch of the old prairie, this spectacular, tall grass still survives quite well. It is often called turkeyfoot because the pattern created by the 3 branches of the seed head looks like the footprint of a wild turkey. Long, narrow leaves turn reddish in fall, and the lower leaves have white, silky hairs. Blooms in August and September. It is a large-volume forage plant, producing 1 to 2½ tons of hay per acre.

HEIGHT: 6 to 7 feet.
RANGE: Throughout Midwest.

Little Bluestem

Little Bluestem
(*Andropogon scoparium*)

This habitant of dry, solid bluffs and high ground doesn't require as much moisture as its larger cousin big bluestem. Leaves are 4 to 10 inches long and are sometimes bluish green. Numerous spikes bear flowers July through September.

HEIGHT: 1 to 4 feet.
RANGE: Illinois, Missouri, Minnesota.

Broom Sedge

Broom Sedge
(*Andropogon virginicus*)

A common invader of overgrazed or disrupted prairie, it grows in tufts, with leaves 6 to 12 inches long and very hairy on upper surface, where they attach to the stem. The stalk bears 2 to 4 fingerlike flower clusters enclosed by leaves and topped with a tuft of white hairs. Blooms September to October. The stem can be split and used in the manufacture of brooms and brushes.

HEIGHT: 1 to 3 feet.
RANGE: Illinois, Indiana, Missouri.

Prairie Three Awn

Prairie Three Awn
(Aristida oligantha)

This grass has typical narrow, flat, smooth leaves that taper to a point. There is a loose array of flowers in 1-flowered spikelets at the top of the stalk. Seeds have bristles up to 3 inches long.

HEIGHT: 1 to 2 feet.
RANGE: Illinois, Indiana, Missouri, Iowa.

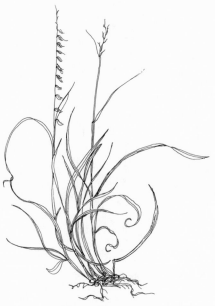

Side Oats Grama

Side Oats Grama
(*Bouteloua curtipendula*)

This grass of glades and dry prairie has leafy tufts with narrow leaf blades, which are hairy with bumps along the edges. The flower blooms 1-sided on an erect stalk in the form of numerous hanging spikes June through August.

HEIGHT: 2 feet.
RANGE: Illinois, Missouri.

Bromegrass

Bromegrass
(*Bromus kalmii*)

This plant will grow in woods and thickets, as well as in wet prairie. Typical leaf blades are 2½ to 7 inches long and slightly hairy. Six to 10 flowered spikelets bloom on slender branches July through August.

HEIGHT: 1½ to 3 feet.
RANGE: Illinois, Missouri.

Nodding Wild Rye

Nodding Wild Rye
(Elymus canadensis)

A grass of roadsides and upland prairies, this member of the barley tribe is usually not found in a mature prairie. It starts to grow in autumn and stays green through the winter. The bluish green leaf is 4 to 12 inches long. Flowers bloom July through August on a broad, stout, bristly spike.

HEIGHT: 4½ feet.
RANGE: Illinois, Missouri.

June Grass

June Grass
(Koeleria cristata)

This native of high, dry prairie and open woods is a typical grass with narrow leaf blades. A tight flower bundle in a spike is at the end of a stem.

HEIGHT: 20 inches.
RANGE: Minnesota, Ontario, Wisconsin.

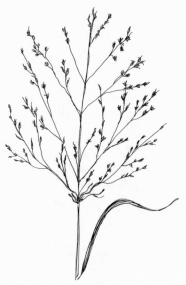

Switch Grass

Switch Grass

(Panicum virgatum)

This erect, coarse grass grows in clumps starting in early April. It matures before other prairie grasses. The leaf is smooth and characteristically narrow, with a tuft of hairs at its junction with the stem. Flowers bloom in a dense, elongated cluster at the top of the stalk July and August.

HEIGHT: 5 feet.
RANGE: Illinois, Missouri, Indiana.

Indian Grass

Indian Grass
(Sorghastrum nutans)

This typical grass of roadside and prairie grows in a tall, coarse clump. Leaf blades are smooth or slightly hairy. A plumelike spike blooms dark brown at the tip of a stem with coarse hairs August and September. The grass is nutritious forage.

HEIGHT: 7 feet.
RANGE: Illinois, Missouri.

Baldgrass

Baldgrass
(Sporobulus neglectus)

This grass is a pioneer of waste ground, though it is found in prairie and open woods, also. The leaf is typically narrow and smooth but somewhat hairy at base. The flower blooms July and August in a typical grass spike but does not have the usual hairs or bristles that other grasses generally have on their flowers.

HEIGHT: 1½ to 2½ feet.
RANGE: Illinois, Iowa, Missouri, Wisconsin, Minnesota.

Trees

Rough-leaved Dogwood

Rough-leaved Dogwood
(*Cornus drummondii*)

This is a border tree between prairies and woods, though it grows elsewhere, too. It has egg-shaped leaves, 2 to 5 inches long, with 3 to 5 pairs of veins. White, 4-petaled blossoms bloom May through June and produce white, round berries May through June. The bark is brown, with twigs tinged red. The hard, heavy wood is used for tool handles.

HEIGHT:　Up to 30 feet at maturity.
RANGE:　Throughout Midwest.

Eastern Red Cedar

Eastern Red Cedar
(*Juniperus virginiana*)

A very adaptable tree, this conifer of the juniper family can be found in dry soil, as well as wet. It prefers open fields and sunshine. Three-sided, scalelike needles, up to ¾ of an inch long, grow in pairs in a row along each of the 4 sides of the twigs. The tree produces a hard, globular, whitish-to-blackish-green berry. The bark is gray to reddish brown and fibrous. The reddish, aromatic wood is used in cedar chests and cabinets.

HEIGHT: 40 to 50 feet at maturity.
RANGE: Throughout Midwest except upper Ontario.

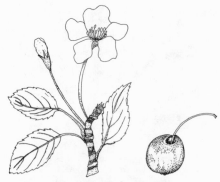

Prairie Crab Apple

Prairie Crab Apple
(Malus coronaria)

As its name implies, this small, thicket-forming tree of prairie and woodland borders produces an edible but bitter apple September to November. The fruit is yellow green and 1 inch in diameter. Oval-shaped leaves, about 3 inches long, have saw-toothed edges and occasionally shallow lobes. A 5-petaled, showy flower blooms on a long stalk, usually in clusters of 3 or more, March through June. Blossoms are white and very fragrant. The bark varies from a gray to red brown. The hard, durable wood is used in tool handles.

HEIGHT: Up to 25 feet.
RANGE: Throughout Midwest.

Bur Oak

Bur Oak
(Quercus macrocarpa)

This oak is common to both the rich, wet soils of bottomlands and the dry prairie edges. It was a prairie pioneer because its thick, corky bark gave it a better chance to survive the scorching fires that raced through the wild prairie. With its deep taproot, it is also very drought resistant. It has the largest leaves of all the oaks—up to 14 inches long. They are dark green and egg shaped with lobes. The largest acorns also are borne on this tree, being 1½ inches in diameter, with a deep cup covered with loose, bushy fringe. The wood is used in cabinets, as fence posts, and as fuel.

HEIGHT: Up to 120 feet.
RANGE: Throughout Midwest.

Shrubs

Redroot

Redroot
(*Ceanothus americanus*)

WHITE/YELLOW

This shrub, also called New Jersey tea, prefers dry, open prairies and thickets. Leaves are oval shaped, sharp tipped with a saw-toothed edge, and 1 to 3 inches long. Small, white and yellow flowers bloom in dense, oblong clusters May through July. The leaves were used as a tea substitute by the colonial troops during the American Revolution. It is one of the only members of the bean family to grow nitrogen-fixing nodules in its roots.

HEIGHT: Up to 4 feet.
RANGE: Illinois, Indiana.

Kalm's St.-John's-Wort

Kalm's St.-John's-Wort   YELLOW
(Hypericum kalmianum)

This shrub grows in dry, sandy soils. Clusters of leafy shoots often grow from the junction of leaf and stem. Leaves are smooth edged, 1 to 2 inches long, and set in pairs on the stalk. Five-petaled, bright yellow flowers bloom in clusters July through September.

HEIGHT: 1 to 4 feet.

RANGE: Shores of Great Lakes and sand prairie throughout Midwest.

Prairie Willow

Prairie Willow   WHITE
(*Salix humilis*)

A member of the willow tree family that has
adapted as a shrub, it is similar to a pussy
willow in appearance and prefers dry thickets
and open prairie. It has narrow, wedge-shaped
leaves, 2 inches long, with a smooth edge.
They are gray green on top and gray and hairy
underneath. White flowers bloom March
through June.

HEIGHT: Up to 13 feet.
RANGE: Throughout Midwest.

Common Elderberry

Common Elderberry

WHITE

(Sambucus canadensis)

This shrub is found at prairie and field edges. The leaf has a coarse-toothed edge and is made up of 5 to 11 elliptical leaflets, which are 4 to 11 inches long. Small, dense, flat-topped clusters, 5 to 8 inches across, bloom with white flowers June through July. A berrylike fruit, produced August through October, is small, juicy, purple black, and edible.

HEIGHT: 3 to 13 feet.
RANGE: Throughout Midwest.

3

The Woodlands

Two kinds of woodlands are found in the midwestern landscape: the evergreen forest of coniferous (cone-bearing) trees stretching down from the north, and the broadleaf hardwood forest pushing in from the east and south. These two distinct forests come together at the center, creating a dramatic mixture throughout Minnesota, Michigan, and Wisconsin. The flowers that grow on the forest floors are the same, and all are brought together in this section.

The broadleaf hardwood forest ranges from the East Coast west to the Mississippi River valley. A thin band of this forest stretches farther west through the Ozark region of southern Missouri and into Arkansas.

The trees of this forest are called deciduous, from the Latin *decidere,* meaning to cut off or fall off. The leaves of deciduous trees fall off each autumn. This, among other things, distinguishes them from the conifers, which hold their spike leaves, or needles, year round.

Most of the eastern and much of the midwestern United States was once covered by this vast broadleaf forest. In Illinois and Indiana it abutted the prairie. Even on the prairie, the forest kept a toehold in the deep, quiet river bottoms. In the vast shadows created by these hardwood giants lived the American Indian. Only the native American and early settlers saw the forest primeval on the continent, a forest that had existed for about 70 million years with little or no change. Long before the dawn of man, oaks, elms, maples, and sycamores were spreading their limbs to the midwestern sunshine. Aside from biotic fluctuations created during various glacial advances, the forests have stood the test of time.

The broadleaf forest thrives on a moderate climate with an evenly distributed annual rainfall. Moisture comes from the Gulf of Mexico and the Atlantic Ocean during the growing seasons, while the furious north and northwest winds of winter carry moisture in the form of snow from the Great Lakes and points northward.

These deciduous trees are characterized by heavily branched, broad, leafy crowns. They have soft, green leaves, usually fairly wide, and a deep-running taproot. Their seeds are enclosed in fruits, nuts, or berries.

Contrary to popular belief, the first frost does not cause the leaves to drop. The leaves are slowly choked off at the base of the leaf-stalk by a corky substance that gathers slowly and shuts off the leaf. The process begins in late summer and is triggered by the shortening of the days.

Over thousands of years the falling leaves have built up a rich humus soil on the forest floor. This haven for a myriad of plant and animal life comes alive each spring. A succession of delicate flowers begins to grow in early March when sunlight first warms the forest floor after the last snow has melted. Later, after buds have turned to leaves on the trees, flowers that thrive in shade arrive. Successive blooming periods last until waning September finds the new leaf fall re-covering the forest floor with a harmony of golds, reds, and browns.

The woods of the north, dominated by conifers, are rooted in a shallower, more acidic soil than the hardwood forest. The triangular-shaped, green spires of the conifers are etched beautifully into the winter landscape. They are trees that are much, much

older than the hardwoods. They are direct
descendants of trees that grew 250 million
years ago. These trees can survive the rigors
of the northern climate quite well because
they hold a thick, resinous sap that insulates
the leaves and branches.

Because little sunlight penetrates the thick
crowns of the trees, plant life on the forest
floor is quite limited. In addition, long, harsh
winters with thick snow cover further limit
the development of plant life beneath the
trees.

The conifers are straight and tall, bearing
needles and cones. The cones are actually
clusters of naked seeds. The trees don't have
large taproots but instead have a woven mat
of smaller roots and rootlets.

The northern forest is dominated by black
and white spruce, with much balsam fir, larch,
and arborvitae. It ranges from northern
Ontario into Minnesota, Wisconsin, and Michigan,
blending with the hardwood forest
farther south. Most traces of the northern
forest disappear completely at the northern
borders of Illinois, Indiana, and Iowa.

Flowers

Miterwort

Miterwort   WHITE
(Mitella diphylla)

This plant grows in rich-soiled woods. Heart-shaped, lobed, and toothed leaves grow on stalks at the stem's base. Two leaves with no stalks grow near the flower spray. An inflorescence of small, slender, spikelike flowers with fringed petals bloom April through May.

HEIGHT: 18 inches.
RANGE: Throughout Midwest.

Spotted Wintergreen

Spotted Wintergreen   WHITE
(*Chimaphila maculata*)

This plant prefers evergreen woods. Toothed
leaves have a pale pattern in the middle. They
vein and taper to a point and radiate from the
same point on the stem. Very fragrant, waxy,
nodding flowers bloom along one side of the
stem June through August.

HEIGHT: 10 inches.
RANGE: Upper Midwest.

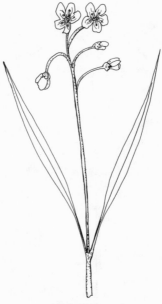

Spring Beauty

Spring Beauty
(Claytonia virginica)

WHITE/PINK

Eastern oak woodlands are the most common habitat of this delicate flower. Smooth, linear leaves are attached midway up the stem. A 5-petaled flower blooms on stalks at right angles to the stem March through May. Each plant may have from 2 to 40 flowering stems.

HEIGHT: 6 to 12 inches.
RANGE: Throughout Midwest.

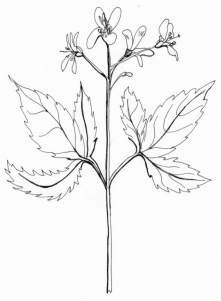

Pepperwort

Pepperwort
WHITE
(Dentaria diphylla)

This member of the mustard family favors
rich, moist woods. A pair of nearly opposite
stem leaves, each divided into 3 broad, toothed
leaflets, grows above long-stalked leaves at the
base. They taste like watercress. A 4-petaled
flower blooms April through June.

HEIGHT: 8 to 16 inches.
RANGE: Upper Midwest.

Dutchman's-breeches

Dutchman's-breeches
(Dicentra cucullaria)

WHITE/PINK

Although a once common member of the poppy family, this plant is becoming scarce. It grows in rich-soiled woodlands and needs plenty of shade. Leaves at the base of the plant are pale green and delicately divided into variable segments. The leafless flowering stem has arching sprays of waxy, yellow-tipped blossoms April through May.

HEIGHT: 1 foot.
RANGE: Upper Midwest.

Wood Strawberry

Wood Strawberry   WHITE
(*Fragaria vesca*)

This plant of dry upland woods and grassy
slopes is very similar to the wild strawberry.
Flowers with 5 round petals bloom in a flat
cluster May through August. They produce a
red, edible fruit.

HEIGHT: 3 to 6 inches.
RANGE: Upper Midwest.

White Baneberry

White Baneberry
(Acrae pachypoda)

WHITE

All parts of this plant, which grows in moist, shady woods, are poisonous, particularly its roots and berries. Leaves are divided and sub-divided into leaflets, 1 to 3 inches long, with sharply toothed edges. A very delicate flower with 4 to 10 narrow petals and protruding centers blooms May through June. It produces a cluster of white berries, each with a thick, red stalk and a black spot, or eye.

HEIGHT: 1 to 2 feet.
RANGE: Throughout Midwest.

Wild Leek

Wild Leek   WHITE
(Allium tricoccum)

This woodland plant has 2 or 3 broad, smooth, onion-scented leaves that are 10 inches long. However, they wither before the flowers bloom June through July at the top of the stem supported by a spokelike structure of branchlets. The plant is used for seasoning food.

HEIGHT: 6 to 18 inches.
RANGE: Throughout Midwest.

Wood Anemone

Wood Anemone   WHITE/PINK
(*Anemone quinquefolia*)

Although a delicate, short plant of hardwood forests, it is long lived, with roots that withstand bitter cold. Leaves on long stalks are divided into 3 or 5 sections and have lightly toothed edges. A single flower with 4 to 9 petallike sepals blooms April through June.

HEIGHT: 4 to 8 inches.
RANGE: Upper Midwest.

Rue Anemone

Rue Anemone

WHITE

(Anemonella thalictroides)

This delicate woodland flower is short. It has 2 or 3 flowers on a slender stalk above a set of leaves that radiate from the stalk. Six petal-like, white sepals form the blossom that blooms March through May.

HEIGHT: 4 to 8 inches.
RANGE: Upper Midwest.

American Spikenard

American Spikenard   WHITE
(*Aralia racemosa*)

Rich-soiled woods are the preferred habitat of
this branching plant with a smooth, blackish
stem. The leaf is divided and then subdivided
into 6 to 21 heart-shaped leaflets and is sometimes 3 feet long. Round, stalked clusters of
small flowers bloom June through August and
produce a dark purple berry in September.

HEIGHT: 3 to 5 feet.
RANGE: Throughout Midwest.

Sharp-lobed Hepatica

Sharp-lobed Hepatica

WHITE/PINK/BLUE

(Hepatica acutiloba)

/LAVENDER

This member of the buttercup family prefers upland woods and rocky slopes. A 3-to-7-lobed, pointed leaf grows from the base. The flower is made up of 6 to 10 petallike sepals and blooms 1 flower per stalk.

HEIGHT: 4 to 9 inches.
RANGE: Upper Midwest.

Downy Rattlesnake Plantain

Downy Rattlesnake Plantain   WHITE
(*Goodyera pubescens*)

This orchid of oak or pine forests is small.
Broad leaves radiate from the base of a woolly stem and have a checkered pattern created
by light green lines. Very small flowers bloom
spikelike in a densely clustered cylinder shape
July through August.

HEIGHT: 6 to 16 inches.
RANGE: Upper Midwest.

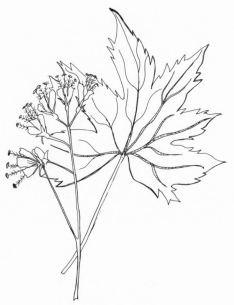

Broad-leaved Waterleaf

Broad-leaved Waterleaf
(Hydrophyllum canadense)

WHITE/PURPLE

Named for light markings on its leaves that look like watermarks, this plant grows in shady, damp woods. Multilobed, maplelike leaves have jagged teeth. Flowers bloom June through July in radiating clusters on stalks attached to the stem below the leaves.

HEIGHT: 1 to 3 feet.
RANGE: Throughout Midwest.

Canada Mayflower

Canada Mayflower   WHITE
(*Maianthemum canadense*)

This plant of woods and woodland clearings, also called wild lily of the valley, sometimes forms a carpet of green leaves on the forest floor. Two oval, pointed leaves wrap around the stem at its notched base. Tiny, 4-pointed, fragrant flowers are stalked and bloom in small clusters May through July. A speckled white turning to red berry is produced.

HEIGHT: 3 to 6 inches.
RANGE: Throughout Midwest.

Indian Pipe

Indian Pipe
WHITE

(Monotropa uniflora)

Since this unusual plant lacks chlorophyll, it is not green but whitish. It lives on dead or living organic material in the soil of shady woods and often grows near mushrooms. Leaves look like scales and grow tightly along the stem. The single, nodding, translucent, pipelike flower turns black after blooming June through September.

HEIGHT: 4 to 10 inches.
RANGE: Throughout Midwest.

Showy Orchis

Showy Orchis   WHITE AND PURPLE
(*Orchis spectabilis*)

This orchid is much stouter than others of its
family and prefers rich soils in moist hardwood forests. A showy arrangement of 2 to 15
flowers grows on short stalks and attaches to
the stem. The flower has a lower lip and a
hood created by arrangements of petals and
modified leaves. Blooms April through June.

HEIGHT: 4 to 12 inches.
RANGE: Throughout Midwest.

Common Wood Sorrel

Common Wood Sorrel
WHITE/PINK
(Oxalis montana)

This plant is a low, creeping woodland plant.
The leaf has 3 cloverlike leaflets. The flower
has 5 notched petals and is veined with pink.
Blooms May through July.

HEIGHT: 3 to 4 inches.
RANGE: Upper Midwest.

Mayapple

Mayapple   WHITE
(Podophyllum peltatum)

This common flower of open woods grows as either a single large, roundish, and deeply lobed leaf at the top of a stalk or as a stem with 2 such leaves and a stalked flower in between. Leaves of an extensive colony look like a carpet floating above the ground. The 6-to-9-petaled flower blooms under the umbrellalike leaves April through June and produces a lemonlike berry with poisonous seeds.

HEIGHT: 12 to 18 inches.
RANGE: Throughout Midwest.

Early Saxifrage

Early Saxifrage   WHITE
(Saxifraga virginiensis)

Dry woods and rocky crevices are the habitat
of this plant. Oval-shaped leaves, 1 to 3 inches
long, with a saw-toothed edge are nearly as
wide as they are long. They grow in a radial
arrangement from the base of a sticky, hairy
stem. A 5-petaled, fragile flower blooms in
terminal clusters March through May.

HEIGHT: 4 to 10 inches.
RANGE: Upper Midwest.

False Solomon's Seal

False Solomon's Seal   WHITE
(*Smilacina racemosa*)

This plant grows in rich-soiled or sandy-soiled woodlands. The arrangement of the leaves is very similar to that of the true Solomon's seal. Leaves are oval shaped, pointed, 2½ to 6 inches long, broad, and glossy. Fragrant flowers clustered at the tip of the stem bloom May through July. A whitish berry is produced with brown-to-ruby-red speckles.

HEIGHT: 1 to 3 feet.
RANGE: Throughout Midwest.

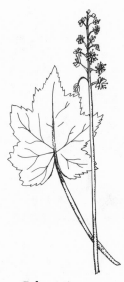

False Miterwort

False Miterwort   WHITE
(Tiarella cordifolia)

Growing via long runners in rich, moist-soiled woods, this plant, also called foamflower, can spread quickly. Large, stalked leaves, with numerous hairs on the upper side, grow from the plant's base. Flowers have narrow petals and bloom in clusters at the end of each stem April through May.

HEIGHT: 6 to 12 inches.
RANGE: Upper Midwest.

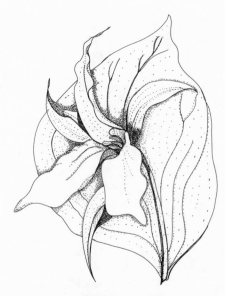

Large-flowered Trillium

Large-flowered Trillium   WHITE/PINK/GREEN
(*Trillium grandiflorum*)

This member of the lily family grows in rich, moist woodland soils. Three broad, stalkless leaves are attached to a thin, smooth stem, which is purplish at its base. A pretty, stalked flower with petals up to 3 inches long that turn pink with age blooms April through June. A bright red berry with 6 ridges is produced.

HEIGHT: 6 to 18 inches.
RANGE: Upper Midwest.

Bluebead

Bluebead　　　YELLOW/GREEN/GREENISH WHITE
(Clintonia borealis)

This flower of rich woods or open slopes is
particular about temperature, growing only in
cooler areas. Two or 3 broad, shining leaves
grow around the base. Six-pointed, nodding,
bell-like flowers bloom in threes on a leafless
stem June through July and produce blue berries.

HEIGHT:　6 to 16 inches.
RANGE:　Upper Midwest.

Yellow Lady's-slipper

Yellow Lady's-slipper   YELLOW
(*Cypripedium calceolus*)

A variable plant, it can grow in dry woods or
bogs. Beautiful, fragrant flowers having
twisted petals and a saclike lip bloom 1 or 2 on
a stem May through July. Petals and sepals are
greenish or purplish brown.

HEIGHT: 2 feet.
RANGE: Throughout Midwest.

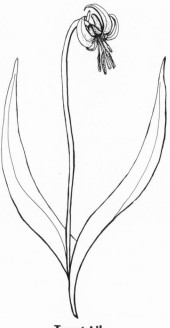

Trout Lily

Trout Lily   YELLOW
(*Erythronium americanum*)

This member of the lily family prefers moist, rich-soiled woods and lots of sunshine. It has 2 broad, mottled basal leaves that are 4 to 8 inches long. A nodding, bell-like, 6-pointed flower blooms March through May.

HEIGHT: 4 to 10 inches.
RANGE: Upper Midwest.

Woodland Sunflower

Woodland Sunflower   YELLOW
(Helianthus divaricatus)

This is a daisylike flower of dry thickets and open woods. Thick, slender leaves are rough on top and hairy underneath. They are attached in pairs to a smooth stem by short stalks. The flower is made up of many petal-like rays and blooms July through October.

HEIGHT: 2 to 6½ feet.
RANGE: Throughout Midwest.

True Solomon's Seal

True Solomon's Seal   YELLOW/GREEN
(Polygonatum biflorum)

The arrangement of flowers distinguishes this flower of open woods and thickets from false Solomon's seal. This plant has pairs of flowers dangling from the junction of the leaves and stem, and the other has flowers at the top of the stem. Oval-shaped leaves are attached directly to the stem. Blooms May through June and produces a blue-black berry.

HEIGHT: 1 to 3 feet.
RANGE: Throughout Midwest.

Common Cinquefoil

Common Cinquefoil
(Pontentilla simplex)

YELLOW

Resembling the wild strawberry, this plant grows in dry woods and fields. Flowers and leaves grow from runners, or spreading stems, on separate stalks. The leaf radiates in 5 parts and is toothed at the base. A 5-petaled, buttercuplike flower blooms April through June. Roots can be eaten like a potato. It is also used in lotions, gargles, and syrups.

HEIGHT: 6 to 20 inches.
RANGE: Upper Midwest.

Zigzag Goldenrod

Zigzag Goldenrod
(Solidago flexicaulis)

YELLOW

Just one of many goldenrod species found in woods, this is named after the zigzag structure of its stem. Attached to the stem are broad, pointed, sharply tooth-edged leaves on long stalks. Flowers bloom in small clusters at the junction of stem and leaf July through October.

HEIGHT: 4 feet.
RANGE: Throughout Midwest.

Trailing Arbutus

Trailing Arbutus   PINK/WHITE
(*Epigaea repens*)

Because of its beauty and fragrance, this
member of the heath family is becoming rare.
It prefers sandy-soiled conifer woods. Leaves
are oval, leathery, hairy, and always green.
The tubular, 5-lobed flower blooms in clusters
March through May.

HEIGHT   1 foot.
RANGE: Upper Midwest.

Pink Lady's-slipper

Pink Lady's-slipper
(Cypripedium acaule)

PINK

The most common lady's-slipper, this showy member of the orchid family grows in a diverse number of habitats, ranging from dry woods to wetland bogs. The single flower has a pink lip with red veins and brown lateral petals that stick out on either side. Blooms May through June.

HEIGHT: 6 to 15 inches.
RANGE: Upper Midwest.

Wild Geranium

Wild Geranium   PINK
(Geranium maculatum)

Although this hardy plant thrives in a variety of habitats, it prefers woods, thickets, and shady roadsides. Two short-stalked leaves with 5 hairy parts grow on a long stem. The other leaves are on long stalks. The 5-petaled, showy flower with a long, beaklike structure extending from its center blooms April through June. Roots are used to make a medicinal astringent.

HEIGHT: 2 feet.
RANGE: Upper Midwest.

Eastern Columbine

Eastern Columbine   ORANGE/RED
(Aquilegia canadensis)

Very adaptable, this member of the buttercup
family prefers rocky woods and slopes but will
grow well in moist or dry soil and in sun or
shade. Leaves are divided and subdivided into
threes. A drooping, 5-petaled tubed flower
with long, curved appendages, or spurs,
blooms on a stalk April through July.

HEIGHT: 1 to 2 feet.
RANGE: Throughout Midwest.

Wood Violet

Wood Violet

BLUE

(*Viola palmata*)

This pretty flower of woodlands has a 5-petaled blossom, with the fifth petal forming a lower spur. It has a yellow center. Blooms April through May.

HEIGHT: 4 to 12 inches.
RANGE: Throughout Midwest.

Jacob's Ladder

Jacob's Ladder   BLUE
(Polemonium reptans)

Rich-soiled woods and bottomlands are the habitat of this plant. Paired leaves are divided by sharp, pointed leaflets, 5 to 15 in number. Five-petaled, bell-like flowers bloom in small, terminal clusters April through June.

HEIGHT: 12 inches.
RANGE: Throughout Midwest.

Tall Bellflower

Tall Bellflower
BLUE
(*Campanula americana*)

Although it prefers the rich soil of woods and thickets, this plant can also be found along roadsides. Leaves are oval or lance shaped, with the lower ones growing on a short stalk. Their base is tapered. A 5-petaled flower with widely spread, pointed lobes blooms on a spike at the top of the stem June through August.

HEIGHT: 4 or more feet.
RANGE: Throughout Midwest.

Harebell

Harebell   BLUE
(Campanula rotundifolia)

A fairly adaptable plant, this flower can be
found on rock ledges and in dry places and
woods. A 5-petaled, hanging, bell-like, blossom blooms June through September.

HEIGHT: 2 feet.
RANGE: Throughout Midwest.

Closed Gentian

Closed Gentian

BLUE

(Gentiana andrewsii)

This is a plant of wet woods and meadows. Paired, smooth leaves are attached directly to the stem. Petals of the flower stay closed, forming a tube shape, and are covered by a fringed, whitish membrane. Flowers bloom in clusters at the top of the stem and at the junctions of leaves and stems August through October.

HEIGHT: 1 to 2 feet.
RANGE: Ontario, Missouri.

Virginia Cowslip

Virginia Cowslip   BLUE
(Mertensia virginica)

This plant grows in rich-soiled woods and
bottomlands. Oval-shaped, smooth, strongly
veined leaves are attached to a smooth, succulent stem. Nodding, trumpetlike, 5-petaled
flowers grow in clusters at the top of the stem.
Buds are pink. Blooms March through May.

HEIGHT: 1 to 2 feet.
RANGE: Upper Midwest.

Common Blue Phlox

Common Blue Phlox   VIOLET/BLUE
(Phlox divaricata)

Rich-soiled, open woods are the habitat of this plant. Leafy shoots persist through winter. A 5-petaled flower radiating from the tip of the stem above wedge-shaped leaves blooms April through June.

HEIGHT: 10 to 20 inches.
RANGE: Throughout Midwest.

Alumroot

Alumroot

GREEN/RED

(Heuchera americana)

This is a widespread and variable plant of shady, dry woods. It has a multiple-lobed, maplelike leaf. Five-petaled, bell-shaped flowers bloom in drooping clusters from the tips of a short-branched stem. Blooms April through June.

HEIGHT: 2 to 3 feet.
RANGE: Upper Midwest.

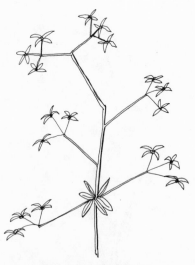

Fragrant Bedstraw

Fragrant Bedstraw   GREENISH WHITE
(*Galium triflorum*)

This woodland plant has leaves radiating in
sets of 6 from a smooth stem. They are rough,
oblong, and fragrant when dried. The American Indian used them for perfume. A 4-petaled
flower blooms in groups of 3 June through
August.

HEIGHT: 4 feet.
RANGE: Throughout Midwest.

Jack-in-the-Pulpit

Jack-in-the-Pulpit   GREEN/PURPLE
(Arisaema atrorubens)

An unusual woodland flower, this plant has a
modified leaf that cups the base and shelters
the top of a flower spike. The overhanging
leaf above the flower acts as a rain hood to
protect the flower for reproductive purposes.
There are 2 leaves divided into 3 lobes.
Blooms April through June. Scarlet berries are
borne in a cluster. Indians used to boil and eat
its peppery bulb.

HEIGHT: 1 to 2 feet.
RANGE: Throughout Midwest.

Ginseng

Ginseng

GREEN

(Panax quinquefolius)

This plant of rich-soiled woods and shady areas is not as common as it once was. Leaves are palmlike and divided into 5 segments, each stalked and attached to the tip of the stem. A small, round cluster of greenish flowers later produces a cluster of red berries. The Chinese use the root as a medicine.

HEIGHT: 1 to 2 feet.
RANGE: Upper Midwest.

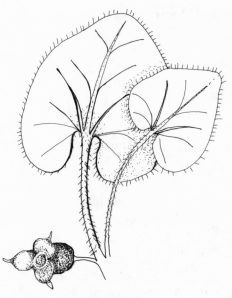

Wild Ginger

Wild Ginger   BROWN
(*Asarum canadense*)

This plant prefers damp areas in rich-soiled
woods. A single cup-shaped flower with 3 red-
brown calyx lobes blooms at ground level
between 2 leaf stalks April through May. The
root can make a refreshing tea or be used as
seasoning in place of commercial ginger.

HEIGHT: 6 to 12 inches.
RANGE: Upper Midwest.

Trees (Deciduous)

Box Elder

Box Elder
(Acer negundo)

This member of the maple family is the only one with leaves divided into leaflets. The paired opposite leaves have 3 or 5 leaflets, which are tooth edged, sometimes with 3 lobes, and 2 to 4 inches long. Clusters of yellow green flowers bloom April through May. A V-shaped, winged seed is borne in loose, drooping clusters September through October.

HEIGHT: 40 to 50 feet.
RANGE: Throughout Midwest except north- ern Ontario.

Sugar Maple

Sugar Maple
(Acer saccharum)

This is the maple syrup tree. A hollow tube is set in the trunk's side in late winter or early spring, and a small quantity of sap is collected and then boiled down to make maple sugar. There are 5 slightly wavy-toothed points on the leaves, which are 2 to 10 inches long. They turn bright yellow or orange in autumn. Greenish yellow flowers bloom April to June and generally appear before the leaves. The winged seeds occur in pairs June through September and resemble a horseshoe. The heavy, beautifully grained wood is used in quality furniture.

HEIGHT: 60 to 80 feet at maturity.
RANGE: Throughout Midwest.

Tree of Heaven

Tree of Heaven
(Ailanthus altissima)

This tree, imported as an ornamental, has reached proportions of infestation that make it a weed. Featherlike leaves, 12 to 24 inches long, have 11 to 41 leaflets, which are smooth edged except for a pair of teeth near the base. Small, clustered, foul-smelling, yellowish flowers bloom June through July. Large clusters of winged seeds are borne September into the winter.

HEIGHT: 80 to 100 feet.
RANGE: Lower Midwest.

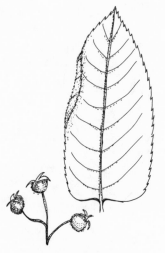

Downy Juneberry

Downy Juneberry
(Amelanchier arborea)

This small tree prefers rich upland soils on forest ridges. Leaves are oval shaped, 2 to 4 inches long, and smooth, with silky hairs along veins. Very pretty, delicate, white flowers appear March through June before the leaves come out. An edible, reddish purple berry is borne June through August.

HEIGHT: 20 to 40 feet at maturity.
RANGE: Throughout Midwest.

Pawpaw

Pawpaw
(Asimina triloba)

This is a smaller tree that grows in the shadow of bottomland hardwood forests. Smooth-edged, tapering leaves are 6 to 12 inches long. Six-petaled flowers, varying in color from pale green to brown or maroon, bloom in the spring and produce 3-to-5-inch-long, edible, bananalike berries. Twigs are covered with rusty red hairs. The trunk is thin and smooth.

HEIGHT: Up to 20 feet.
RANGE: Throughout Midwest.

Yellow Birch

Yellow Birch
(Betula lutea)

A tree of cool, moist forest, this birch is similar to others of the Midwest. Oval-shaped leaves with saw-toothed edges are 1 to 5 inches long and have a wintergreen aroma when crushed. The silver gray bark peels horizontally in papery strips. Twigs and new-growth bark are an amber yellow. The heavy, strong wood is used in flooring and furniture.

HEIGHT: 60 to 70 feet.
RANGE: Throughout Midwest.

Black Birch

Black Birch
(Betula lenta)

This tree prefers the slopes of deep, cool ravines near the shores of the Great Lakes. Smooth, oval-shaped leaves are 1 to 6 inches long and have double saw-toothed edges. The bark is black with thin, horizontal stripes. Wintergreen oil, a common medicinal preparation, is distilled from parts of this tree.

HEIGHT: 50 to 70 feet.
RANGE: Ontario and Great Lakes area.

Paper Mulberry

Paper Mulberry
(Broussonetia papyrifera)

This immigrant tree from Asia prefers thickets and young woods. Leaves have 2 to 3 lobes, are 4 to 11 inches long, have irregularly toothed edges, and are grainy to the touch like sandpaper. They are attached in an alternating pattern to rough, hairy twigs. Flower clusters bloom April through June. A round, semi-fleshy, orange-colored fruit is borne during September. The bark is gray or light brown.

HEIGHT: 20 to 50 feet.
RANGE: Illinois, Indiana, Missouri.

Pignut Hickory

Pignut Hickory
(Carya glabra)

This member of the walnut family prefers dry uplands and is found mixed with other hardwoods. Leaves are 8 to 12 inches long and consist of 5 or 7 spear-shaped leaflets with smooth edges. The hanging, cylindrical male flower, called a catkin, occurs in threes. The reddish brown, husked nut, 1 to 2 inches long, is usually bitter but can be sweet. The bark is dark gray and furrowed on the trunk, which can range from 2 to 4 feet in diameter at maturity.

HEIGHT: 50 to 60 feet.
RANGE: Throughout Midwest.

Pecan

Pecan
(Carya illinoensis)

The largest of the hickory family, it was believed by American Indians to be a manifestation of the Great Spirit. It grows in moist woods and bottomlands. Featherlike leaves, 11 to 20 inches long, have 9 to 17 leaflets that are 4 to 8 inches long. An oblong, reddish brown, edible nut in a thin husk is produced. The hard, strong wood is used for flooring, furniture, and crating.

HEIGHT: 100 to 140 feet.
RANGE: Lower Midwest.

Shagbark Hickory
(Carya ovata)

Although this tree prefers rich bottomland soils, it sprouts readily and can often invade fields and uplands. Leaves are 8 to 14 inches long and composed of 5 lance-shaped leaflets. They are dark yellow green but turn yellow in autumn. The hanging, cylindrical male flower, called a catkin, occurs in threes. A husked nut is borne in the fall. It is edible and an important food for wildlife. The distinctive, gray bark, which curls away from the trunk, gives the tree a shaggy look, hence its name. Historically, the hickory woods of the East paved the way West. The strong, heavy, and flexible wood was used for spokes, hubs, and rims of wagon wheels. Today it is used primarily for hickory chips in barbecuing.

HEIGHT: 70 to 80 feet.
RANGE: Throughout Midwest.

Shagbark Hickory

Black Hickory

Black Hickory
(Carya texana)

This is a small tree of dry woods and dry, stony hillsides. Leaves are 8 to 14 inches long and composed of 7 leaflets that have rust-colored, hairy undersides, unlike other hickories. The hanging, cylindrical male flower, called a catkin, occurs in threes. The 4-sided, globe-shaped nut has a thin husk.

HEIGHT: Up to 25 feet.
RANGE: Lower Midwest.

Mockernut Hickory

Mockernut Hickory
(Carya tomentosa)

This hickory prefers rich, well-drained soils like those of ridges. The leaf is 8 to 15 inches long and made up of 7 to 9 dark yellow green leaflets that are fragrant when crushed. The hanging, cylindrical male flower, called a catkin, occurs in threes. The reddish brown, edible nut, which is borne during October, is globe shaped with a thick, 4-sectioned husk and has a strong scent. The grayish bark becomes rough and furrowed with age on a trunk of up to 3 feet in diameter.

HEIGHT: 50 to 75 feet.
RANGE: Throughout Midwest but comparatively rarer northward.

Catawba Tree

Catawba Tree
(Catalpa speciosa)

This tree prefers rich-soiled bottomlands. Oval-shaped leaves, 8 to 12 inches long, are smooth edged and taper to a point. They are arranged in sets of 2 or 3. A showy, white flower with a notched lower petal blooms May through June. Seeds are borne in a slender, cigar-shaped pod, 10 to 20 inches long, August through November. The bark is deeply ridged.

HEIGHT: 50 to 70 feet.
RANGE: Lower Midwest.

Hackberry

Hackberry
(Celtis occidentalis)

This member of the elm family grows in woods and open places, especially those with moist soils. Egg-shaped leaves are 2 to 4½ inches long and grow in two rows along zigzag branches. Small, greenish flowers bloom singly or in clusters April through May. A sweet, edible, fleshy, purple, berrylike fruit grows on long stalks September through October. The dark grayish bark has warty projections.

HEIGHT: 30 to 50 feet.
RANGE: Throughout Midwest.

Redbud

Redbud
(Cercis canadensis)

This small but beautiful tree that grows in the shadows of the giant hardwoods, like oak and hickory, is a recognized harbinger of spring. The delicate, pink-to-lavender blossoms come out before the leaves, blooming March through May. A reddish pealike seedpod, 2 to 3 inches long, is borne July through August. The tree reaches a diameter of only 10 to 12 inches and has a dark gray bark. Although it is used now as an ornamental, its roots were once used by pioneers to create a natural red dye.

HEIGHT: 15 to 20 feet.
RANGE: Throughout Midwest except northern Ontario.

Yellowwood

Yellowwood
(Cladrastis lutea)

Generally a tree of uplands, it prefers fertile, well-drained soils. Seven to 11 oval-shaped, smooth-edged leaflets, 2 to 4 inches long, make up the leaf. White flowers bloom May through June in large, drooping clusters up to 1 foot in length. A long, flattened pod with 4 to 6 seeds is borne September through October.

HEIGHT: Up to 60 feet.
RANGE: Lower Midwest.

Flowering Dogwood
(*Cornus florida*)

Although it grows in fence rows and on roadsides, this tree is commonly found growing beneath larger hardwoods. Smooth, oval-shaped leaves, 3 to 6 inches long, are bright green but turn red in autumn. The white or pink "petals" of the flower are actually modified leaves. The actual flowers are greenish yellow and are found at the center of the "petals." Blooms April through May. The egg-shaped, berrylike fruit, borne August through November, turns scarlet when ripe. The rough bark looks like alligator skin. When mature, the trunk ranges up to 18 inches in diameter. Although it is used primarily as an ornamental tree today, its hard wood was used for spools, bobbins, and loom shuttles in the past.

HEIGHT: Up to 35 feet.
RANGE: Throughout Midwest.

Flowering Dogwood

Common Persimmon

Common Persimmon
(*Diospyros virginiana*)

Woodlands are just one of the many places where this adaptable member of the ebony family grows. Leaves are oval shaped, 3 to 6 inches long, and smooth edged with a pointed tip. Milky white flowers bloom May through June. Edible, flattened, roundish berries, 1 to 2 inches in diameter, are borne August through November. When ripe, they are orange to blackish purple, with a pulpy flesh inside. Composed of scaly blocks, the bark looks like alligator skin. The wood is blackish.

HEIGHT: 30 to 50 feet.
RANGE: Lower Midwest.

American Beech

American Beech
(Fagus grandifolia)

This granddaddy of American hardwoods can attain a large size and live up to 400 years. It grows in sandy uplands, as well as in rich, mature soils. Egg-shaped leaves with coarsely toothed edges are leathery. Flowers bloom April through May. Prickly, burlike husks contain two small, triangular nuts, which are edible and are favored by many forms of wildlife. The bark is smooth, gray, and distinctive. The wood is used in furniture.

HEIGHT: 70 to 80 feet.

RANGE: Throughout Midwest but less common in Iowa and Minnesota.

White Ash

White Ash
(*Fraxinus americana*)

This, the largest of the ashes, as well as a member of the olive family, prefers mixed woods and clay soils. Featherlike leaves have 5 to 9 stalked leaflets with smooth or slightly toothed edges. Inconspicuous flowers bloom in clusters April through June. A winged, paddle-shaped seed, 1 to 2 inches long, is borne October through November.

HEIGHT: 70 to 80 feet.
RANGE: Throughout Midwest.

Blue Ash

Blue Ash
(Fraxinus quadrangulata)

This ash of upland woods and limestone soils gets its name from the sticky substance of the inner bark, which turns blue when exposed to air. American Indians used this bark to make a blue dye. Leaves are made up of 7 to 11 tooth-edged leaflets in a featherlike arrangement. Flowers bloom in clusters April through May. Twigs are squarish in cross section. The bark is composed of large, scaly, gray plates.

HEIGHT: 50 to 80 feet.
RANGE: Throughout Midwest.

Honey Locust

Honey Locust
(Gleditsia triacanthos)

This tree of woods and wetlands prefers moister soils wherever it grows. It has many stout, branched thorns. Featherlike leaves, 6 to 15 inches long, have 7 to 15 leaflets that vary from egg shaped to spear shaped. Small, fragrant clusters of yellow green flowers bloom May through July. Dark reddish brown seedpods, 10 to 18 inches long, are borne September through February.

HEIGHT: 70 to 80 feet.
RANGE: Throughout Midwest.

Kentucky Coffee Tree

Kentucky Coffee Tree
(*Gymnocladus dioicus*)

This tree is found mixed with other hardwoods in fertile soils, primarily bottomland. It lies dormant for nearly 6 months of each year, leaves appearing late in the spring and falling off early. They are 1 to 3 feet long and have 5 to 9 pairs of leaf branches, each with 8 to 12 leaflets, 1 to 2 inches long, with minute teeth. Whitish flowers bloom May through June in clusters 4 to 12 inches long. Seeds are borne September into winter in a purple, thick-walled pod 6 inches long. The brown seeds were used as a substitute for coffee by early settlers.

HEIGHT: 40 to 80 feet.
RANGE: Lower Midwest.

Butternut

Butternut
(Juglans cinerea)

This tree prefers moist soils of bottomlands. Leaves are made up of featherlike arrangements of 11 to 17 spear-shaped leaflets, which are aromatic when crushed. Oblong nuts are borne in clusters of 2 to 5 in fleshy, green husks covered with sticky hairs. American Indians pressed them to produce oil.

HEIGHT: 50 to 80 feet.
RANGE: Lower Midwest.

Black Walnut

Black Walnut
(Juglans nigra)

This tree needs deep, well-drained soil. It is usually found mixed with white oak, cherry, sugar maple, and white ash. Many plants can't grow on the ground beneath it because of a poisonous substance given off by the roots. Featherlike leaves have 13 to 25 leaflets, 1 to 2 inches long, with finely toothed edges. Large, globe-shaped, edible nuts are borne in green, thick husks about 1½ to 2 inches in diameter. The beautiful, hard wood is highly sought for use in fine furniture.

HEIGHT: Up to 150 feet.
RANGE: Throughout Midwest.

Sweet Gum
(*Liquidambar styraciflua*)

This member of the witch-hazel family prefers bottomland habitats. Five-to-8-inch-long leaves give off the smell of balsam when bruised. They are 5 lobed, almost star shaped, with even-toothed edges. In autumn they turn bright red or yellow. Flowers bloom April through May. Seeds are borne September through November in globe-shaped clusters of capsules, with each capsule containing a single winged seed.

HEIGHT: 50 to 120 feet.
RANGE: Midwest.

Sweet Gum

Tulip Tree
(Liriodendron tulipifera)

This member of the magnolia tree family grows fast in rich, deep soil. It is reportedly the tallest hardwood in America, ranging up to 200 feet in height. Leaves grow on long, slender stems and have 4 main lobes. They are smooth and yellow green in summer but turn to golden yellow in autumn. Flowers are large, 2 inches across, and look waxy. Greenish-yellow and orange tuliplike blossoms bloom May through June. The sweet nectar attracts bees. A whitish, conelike cluster of winged seeds is borne September through November. The tree produces excellent timber.

HEIGHT: 100 to 150 feet or higher.
RANGE: Throughout Midwest but more common in eastern portions.

Tulip Tree

Osage Orange
(*Maclura pomifera*)

Preferring rich soil, this thorny tree grows in dense thickets. It has been used as a living fence to control livestock on farms. Dark green, lustrous leaves are egg shaped with smooth edges and pointed tips. Multiflowered, globe-shaped heads bloom May through June. The green, globe-shaped fruit, 4 to 5 inches in diameter is filled with a milky sap. The stalk is a zigzag of slender twigs, all having sharp spines.

HEIGHT: 4 to 15 feet.
RANGE: Throughout Midwest.

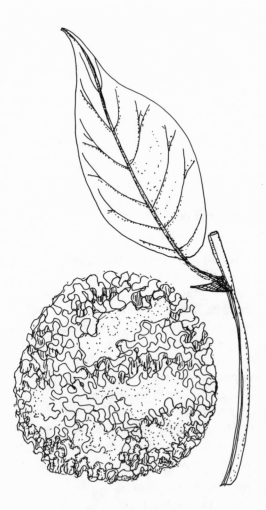

Osage Orange

Cucumber Tree
(Magnolia acuminata)

This tree prefers low hills and bluffs in mature woodlands. Leaves are 6 to 10 inches long and elliptically shaped, with edges that are smooth or slightly wavy. They are dark yellowish green and slightly hairy underneath. Flowers are also large, 2 to 3 inches across, and bloom singly at ends of branches. They are not so conspicuous as other magnolia flowers, being yellow green with no fragrance. A 2½-inch-long, conelike fruit cluster, which releases many bright red seeds on slender green threads, is borne August through October and gives the tree its name.

HEIGHT: 50 to 80 feet.
RANGE: Throughout Midwest except northern Ontario.

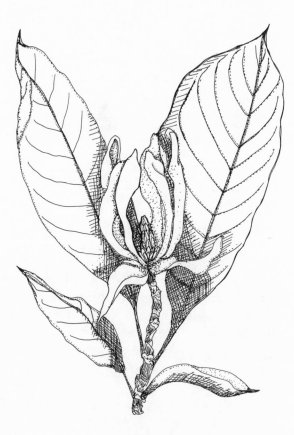

Cucumber Tree

Red Mulberry

Red Mulberry
(Morus rubra)

This is a small tree of rich, well-drained soils. Dark green, heart-shaped leaves are both lobed and unlobed and have coarsely toothed edges. Delicious, red-to-purple berries are abundant through July. The bark is dark with yellow highlights. Twigs exude a milky sap when broken.

HEIGHT: Up to 50 feet.
RANGE: Throughout Midwest.

Ironwood

Ironwood
(Ostrya virginiana)

This small tree is found in upland woods and on rocky bluffs. Egg-shaped leaves with a paperlike texture have double-toothed edges and turn a rust color in autumn. Flowers bloom April through May. The hanging, cylindrical male flower, or catkin, grows in twos or threes the season before, and the female flower blooms in a short spike. A cluster of nutlets is borne in a bladderlike sac resembling hops. The very hard wood is used in axe and hammer handles and in mallets.

HEIGHT: Up to 30 feet.
RANGE: Throughout Midwest.

American Sycamore
(*Platanus occidentalis*)

This monarch of the midwestern forest grows to gigantic proportions and may live 500 to 600 years. It prefers rich river bottoms. Very broad leaves, 6 to 10 inches long, have 3 to 5 main lobes that are coarsely toothed. They are similar to maple leaves but much larger. Ball-shaped clusters of green or red flowers bloom April through June. The mature, brown seed has a plume of hair at its base and occurs in ball-like clusters, also. The mottled, smoothish bark flakes off in pieces. Although the tree grows rapidly, it produces a hard wood with an interlocking grain that has been used in butchers' chopping blocks.

HEIGHT: 50 to 130 feet.
RANGE: Lower Midwest.

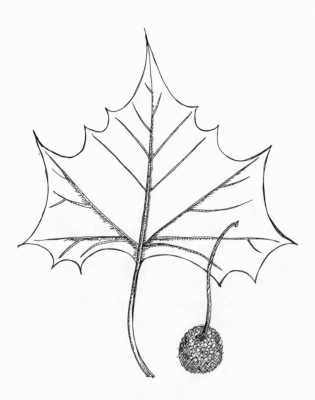

American Sycamore

Big Tooth Aspen

Big Tooth Aspen
(Populus grandidentata)

Relatively short-lived, these pioneer plants readily invade fields and burned areas. They have coarsely toothed, oval-shaped leaves that are 2 to 6 inches long. The soft, white wood is used as paper pulp.

HEIGHT: 30 to 40 feet.
RANGE: Throughout Midwest.

Quaking Aspen

Quaking Aspen
(Populus tremuloides)

Although the tree is short-lived, it roots quickly in cut or burned-over forests and grows rapidly. Egg-shaped, saw-toothed leaves, 2 to 6 inches long, have a leathery texture and turn yellow in the fall. Their seemingly constant quivering has given the tree its name. Seeds have tufts of cottony hair, giving the appearance of tiny parachutes. The smooth bark is either yellow green or light gray. The wood is used for paper pulp.

HEIGHT: 50 feet.
RANGE: Throughout Midwest.

Black Cherry

Black Cherry
(Prunus serotina)

This member of the rose family has oblong
leaves with a blunt, saw-toothed edge. They
give off a distinct bitter almond aroma produced by an acid that can be fatal to cattle.
Long clusters of white flowers bloom April
through May. The fruit is a pea-sized, dark-
red-to-black cherry, which is borne in drooping clusters. It has a winelike, bittersweet
taste. Twigs are reddish brown and the bark
gray. The heavy, hard wood is used in cabi-
netmaking for its fine grain.

HEIGHT: 50 to 60 feet.
RANGE: Throughout Midwest.

White Oak

White Oak
(Quercus alba)

A predominant woodland species, it has many
close relatives with a similar appearance. It
grows in either dry or moist-soiled woods.
Leaves are oblong with rounded lobes and 5 to
9 inches long. The seed is the acorn, which
ripens in one season and has a bowl-shaped
cup that covers about ⅓ of it. The bark on the
short trunk is whitish gray, slightly furrowed,
and scaly. The crown of the tree is often much
wider than high. The heavy, hard wood is
used in flooring and furniture.

HEIGHT: 80 to 100 feet.
RANGE: Throughout Midwest.

Scarlet Oak

Scarlet Oak
(Quercus coccinea)

Dry soils and uplands are the habitat of this tree. Leaves are deeply lobed, with each lobe pointed, and grow 3 to 6 inches in length. They turn a startling shade of red in autumn. The seed is a reddish brown acorn that has a thin, bowl-shaped cup with tight scales and it does not mature until the fall of its second year.

HEIGHT: 70 to 80 feet.
RANGE: Throughout Midwest.

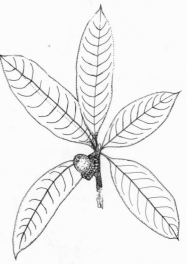

Shingle Oak

Shingle Oak
(Quercus imbricaria)

One of the few oaks with unlobed leaves, this tree has narrow, elliptical, shiny, dark green leaves with smooth or slightly wavy edges and a leathery texture. It grows in bottomlands. The acorn has a cup with thin, hairy scales.

HEIGHT: 50 to 60 feet.
RANGE: Throughout Midwest.

Pin Oak

Pin Oak
(Quercus palustris)

This tree of moist woods and bottomlands has the smallest leaves of all the oaks, just 3 to 5 inches long. They have deep lobes with pointed, bristly tips, or "pins," and turn bright red in the fall. The acorn has a cup that is brown and shallow, almost saucerlike.

HEIGHT: 70 to 80 feet.
RANGE: Throughout Midwest except northern Ontario.

Northern Red Oak

Northern Red Oak
(*Quercus rubra*)

This oak grows rapidly in deep woods that are moist but well drained. Leaves have 7 to 11 upward-pointing, bristle-tipped lobes. They are smooth and yellow green but turn orange and deep red in the fall. The acorn is about 1 inch long, with a saucer-shaped cup.

HEIGHT: 70 to 90 feet.
RANGE: Throughout Midwest.

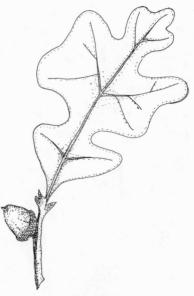

Post Oak

Post Oak
(Quercus stellata)

A smaller oak, this tree grows in poor soil, often on bluffs and ridges. Leaves are leathery and 3 to 8 inches long, with lobes that make them roughly resemble a cross. The small acorn is seated deeply in a bowl-shaped cup.

HEIGHT: 50 to 60 feet.
RANGE: Lower Midwest.

Black Oak

Black Oak
(Quercus velutina)

This oak of dry, rocky ridges has variable, tough, leathery leaves, 5 to 7 inches long, with 5 to 7 bristle-tipped lobes. The acorn is light reddish brown, with a scaly, bowl-shaped cup. The dark bark is bright orange or yellow underneath. The tough wood is used in flooring and crating.

HEIGHT: 50 to 60 feet.
RANGE: Throughout Midwest.

Black Locust
(Robinia pseudoacacia)

This tree grows in fertile, moist soils of woods and fields. It is often planted as a windbreak or to reclaim, by reforestation, abused crop areas. Featherlike leaves, 6 to 12 inches long, are made up of 9 to 19 oval-to-elliptical leaflets that droop and seem to fold up at nightfall. Large, white, fragrant flowers bloom in large, pendant clusters May through June, attracting insects and, consequently, birds. A thin, flat, brown seedpod, 2 to 4 inches long, is borne on the tree September into the spring. The durable wood was often used for fence posts.

HEIGHT: 70 to 80 feet.
RANGE: Throughout Midwest.

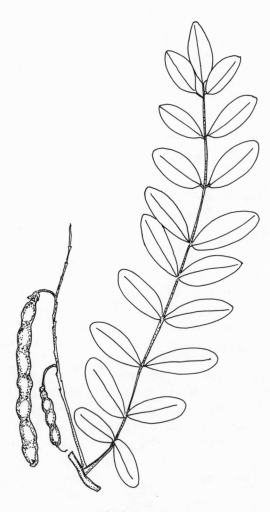

Black Locust

Sassafras
(Sassafras albidum)

This smallish member of the laurel family grows in rich-soiled woods and old fields, quickly invading abandoned agricultural land. Leaves are highly variable, taking several forms on the same tree. They can have 2 or 3 lobes—or none! They are smooth, pointed, heavily veined, and aromatic. Their fall colors are yellow and orange. Yellowish green flowers bloom at the ends of branches in spring and produce clusters of dark-blue berries on thickened, reddish stalks. The bark is very deeply furrowed. The bark of the roots yields an oil that was thought to be a tonic when brewed as tea. It is used today in soap and perfumes and for flavoring.

HEIGHT: 5 to 20 feet.
RANGE: Lower Midwest.

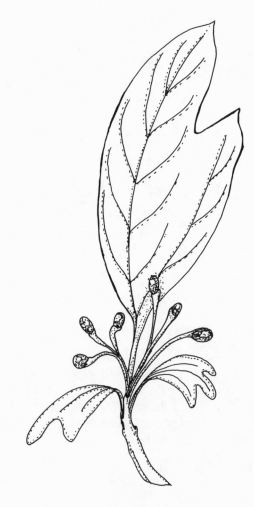

Sassafras

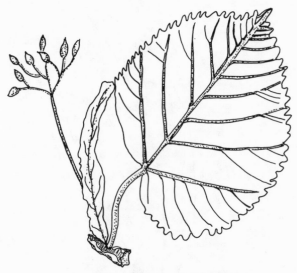

American Basswood (Linden)

American Basswood (Linden)
(Tilia americana)

This tree prefers moist-soiled woods. Heart-shaped leaves, 4 to 8 inches long, are lopsided at the base and have a saw-toothed edge. Small, very fragrant, creamy white flowers bloom June through July.

HEIGHT: 70 to 80 feet.
RANGE: Throughout Midwest.

Winged Elm

Winged Elm
(Ulmus alata)

This unusual tree has twigs with wide, flat, corky ridges, or wings. Spear-shaped leaves have a pointed tip and are 1 to 4 inches long, with very short leafstalks. Small, reddish flowers bloom in drooping, few-flowered clusters in March. Long-stemmed, hanging clusters of seeds follow in March and April.

HEIGHT: 40 to 50 feet.
RANGE: Lower Midwest.

American Elm
(*Ulmus americana*)

Although this tree grows readily in many habitats, it is most common in bottomlands. Used for years as an ornamental, it is the most common shade tree in the United States. However, in recent years its population has been decimated by Dutch elm disease. It can also be readily damaged by heavy snows, which snap its branches. Elliptical leaves, 4 to 6 inches long, have a coarsely double-toothed edge and taper to a point. Flowers bloom in clusters along the stem March through May. Single seeds are also produced in clusters April through May, each being surrounded by a papery wing. The bark is gray and tough. The wood was used in barrels and boxes.

HEIGHT: 50 to 100 feet.
RANGE: Throughout Midwest.

American Elm

Slippery Elm

Slippery Elm
(Ulmus rubra)

This tree's habitat ranges from moist bottom-lands to dry uplands. It can be recognized by rough, hairy twigs and red, hairy buds in winter and spring. Egg-shaped leaves taper to a long, narrow point. Reddish flowers bloom clustered along the branches March through May. The seed also grows in clusters and is surrounded by a thin, papery wing. Reddish brown bark covers a slimy, slippery inner bark, once used as a preventive for scurvy.

HEIGHT: 40 to 60 feet.
RANGE: Michigan, Illinois, Wisconsin, Indi-ana, Missouri.

Trees (Coniferous)

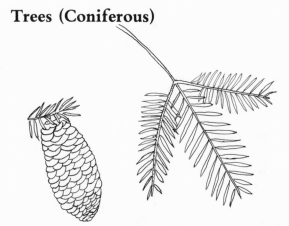

Balsam Fir

Balsam Fir
(Abies balsamea)

This steeple-shaped evergreen of moist northern forests may grow as a matlike shrub. Leaves are flat needles, ⅓ to 1½ inches long, with round tips. A small, conelike flower blooms in late spring. The cones are 1 to 3 inches long and fall apart when ripe. The bark is smooth, with resin blisters. The very fragrant resin, called Canada balsam, is used in miscroscopy to mount specimens on slides. The tree is used for Christmas trees and paper-making.

HEIGHT: 40 to 60 feet.
RANGE: Upper Midwest.

White Spruce
(*Picea glauca*)

This upland conifer has a pyramidlike crown. Stiff, 4-sided, sharply pointed needles are ⅓ to ¾ inch long. Light-brown cones with flexible scales are 1½ to 2 inches long. Most fall when ripe. The wood is used for lumber and paper pulp.

HEIGHT: 40 to 70 feet.
RANGE: Upper Midwest.

Black Spruce
(*Picea mariana*)

Although an upland tree of the north woods, this spruce is also found around cool sphagnum bogs farther south. Leaves are 4-sided, blunt, bluish green needles, ¼ to ½ inch long, on brown, downy twigs. Dull-brown, egg-shaped cones, ½ to 1½ inches long, can remain on the tree for up to 30 years! The slender, spirelike tree is used for Christmas trees and pulpwood.

HEIGHT: 30 to 100 feet.
RANGE: Upper Midwest.

White Spruce   **Black Spruce**

Jack Pine

Jack Pine
(Pinus banksiana)

An evergreen of poor, dry soils, this pine is
scrubby and small. Leaves are needles that
grow very short—¾ to 1⅝ inches long—and in
pairs. Cones usually curve or bulge on one side
and are 1½ to 2 inches long. This tree makes
poor lumber, but it grows on barren land
where other trees can't survive.

HEIGHT: 15 to 40 feet.
RANGE: Throughout Midwest.

Yellow Pine

Yellow Pine
(*Pinus echinata*)

This tree is a conifer of dry, sandy soils of dolomite or sandstone origin. Leaves are evergreen needles, 3 to 5 inches long, in bundles of 2 or 3. They are slender, flexible, and dark green. An egg-shaped cone, 1½ to 3 inches long, is borne for two years, then drops off. The relatively hard wood is used in some cabinetwork and also for fence posts and poles.

HEIGHT: Up to 80 feet.
RANGE: Upper Midwest.

Red Pine (Norway Pine)

Red Pine (Norway Pine)
(*Pinus resinosa*)

A conifer that prefers sandy soils of uplands and ridges, it thrives around the Great Lakes. It is often found growing with eastern white pine. The slender, flexible, dark glossy green needles, 4 to 6 inches long, grow in pairs. Nearly stalkless cones are egg shaped when closed but round when opened. They are light-brown and about 2 inches long. The bark is orange red and flaky when young and covered with large, flat, brown red plates when older. The wood is used in construction and for poles and boxes. The tree is also a popular ornamental.

HEIGHT: 50 to 80 feet.
RANGE: Upper Midwest.

Eastern White Pine

Eastern White Pine
(Pinus strobus)

In the open this evergreen of uplands has a broad, cone-shaped crown. In dense stands, the tall, straight trunks are unbranched for most of their height. Soft, flexible, blue green needles, 3 to 5 inches long, grow in bunches of 5. It is the only 5-needled pine. Spindle-shaped cones, 4 to 8 inches long, are crusted with a whitish, sticky resin. They take two years to mature. The dark bark is deeply furrowed but not scaly. The fine, even-textured wood is easy to work with. Consequently, it is commonly used in construction.

HEIGHT: 80 to 100 feet.
RANGE: Upper Midwest.

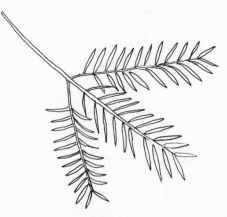

Eastern Hemlock

Eastern Hemlock
(*Tsuga canadensis*)

This graceful evergreen of cold, wet soils and rocky slopes may live for up to 600 years. Soft, flat, narrow needles, ⅓ to ⅔ inch long, are rounded or notched at the tip. They are a shiny dark green on top, with two white stripes underneath. Small, egg-shaped cones, borne in October, shed winged seeds during winter. The bark is dark and rough.

HEIGHT: 60 to 80 feet.
RANGE: Upper Midwest.

Northern White Cedar (Arborvitae)

Northern White Cedar (Arborvitae)
(Thuja occidentalis)

This tree grows in bottomlands of the north woods and on limestone bluffs farther south. Leaves are small, looking like flat, overlapping scales covering the twigs. Bell-shaped cones are ½ inch long. The trunk is used for poles and posts.

HEIGHT: 40 to 50 feet.
RANGE: Upper Midwest.

Shrubs

Devil's-Walking-Stick

Devil's-Walking-Stick   WHITE
(*Aralia spinosa*)

Huge leaves, 2 to 4 feet long, made up of 2 or 3 leaflets, are toothed and pointed. The stalk is thorny. Flowers are numerous 1-inch, flat-topped clusters that bloom July through September. They produce black, fleshy, spherical berries containing 2 to 5 seeds.

HEIGHT: 5 to 15 feet.
RANGE: Illinois, Indiana, Missouri, Iowa, Michigan.

Bearberry

Bearberry   WHITE/PINK
(*Arctostaphylos uva-ursi*)

This trailing shrub of rocky or sandy area is
common locally. However, it is protected by
law in some states. Small, paddle-shaped
leaves are singly attached and green through
all seasons. Egg-shaped flowers bloom in clusters at the ends of branches May through July
and later produce red berries. The bark is
papery and reddish.

HEIGHT: 6 inches.
RANGE: Upper Midwest.

Hawthorns

Hawthorns   WHITE
(*Crataegus*)

This common shrub is very distinctive, with many species that are almost indistinguishable. They have thorny stalks and branches with egg-shaped, sharply toothed leaves. Clusters made up of many flowers bloom during various periods, depending on the species. The fruit is generally a bright red, oblong berry with a thin, succulent flesh popular with wildlife.

HEIGHT: Variable, depending on species.
RANGE: Throughout Midwest.

Virginia Creeper

Virginia Creeper
GREENISH
(Parthenocissus quinquefolia)

This climbing vine with tendrils grows in
woods and thickets. Five to 7 leaflets grow
fanlike from the leafstalk like spokes of a
wheel. They are toothed, 3 to 8 inches long,
and very colorful in autumn. Small clusters of
greenish flowers bloom June through August
and produce blue berries August through February.

HEIGHT: Dependent upon height of object to
which it is attached.
RANGE: Illinois, Minnesota, Indiana, Wisconsin.

Witch Hazel   YELLOW
(Hamamelis virginiana)

An unusual shrub, it blooms when other plants have lost their foliage in the fall. Leaves are oval to elliptical, with a toothed edge and uneven base. Distinctive flowers have long, narrow, ribbonlike petals and bloom September to November. Seeds are borne the following year, August to October, and make a loud noise when popping from the pod. The bark is used to create an extract for medicinal purposes. In the past the forked branches were used as divining rods, which supposedly would vibrate up and down to indicate the presence of underground water supplies.

HEIGHT: 10 to 25 feet.
RANGE: Common throughout Midwest.

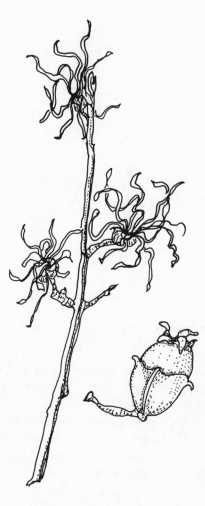

Witch Hazel

Mountain Laurel

Mountain Laurel   PINK/WHITE/PURPLE
(Kalmia latifolia)

This habitant of rocky woods and swamps is a
showy, gnarled shrub that is green through all
seasons. It has flat, leathery, toothless leaves, 2
to 5 inches long, that come to a point. Bowl-
shaped flower clusters, composed of many
cup-shaped flowers, bloom May through July.
Leaves are poisonous to cattle.

HEIGHT: 13 to 15 feet.
RANGE: Indiana, Ontario.

Mountain Ash

Mountain Ash   WHITE
(Sorbus americana)

This shrub of woods and woodland glades has
11 to 17 toothed leaflets, 6 to 9 inches long and
narrow and pointed, arranged in a feather
shape on a leafstalk. Small clusters of flowers
bloom May through June and produce clusters
of red berries in August.

HEIGHT: 40 feet.
RANGE: Illinois, Minnesota, Michigan.

Poison Ivy   WHITE
(Rhus radicans or *Toxicodendron radicans)*

Everyone worries about poison ivy, but few
people can readily recognize it in all its forms.
It is an extremely variable plant, making the
identification difficult and somewhat beyond
the scope of this book. It can occur as a vine,
an erect shrub, or a short sprout. Three leaflets connect at the stalk by their long leaf
stems. They vary in shape and range from 4 to
14 inches in length. The center leaflet is always longer and pointed at the tip. Small
flowers hang clustered from the point where
leaves join the stalk but are sometimes absent.
Ball-shaped, white berries are borne in clusters August to November. An oil produced by
the plant makes every part poisonous.

HEIGHT: 1 to 5 feet.
RANGE: Throughout Midwest.

Poison Ivy

Blackberry

Blackberry   WHITE
(Rubus allegheniensis)

This prickly, rambling shrub favors woodland
thickets. There are 122 species in North
America, all very similar. Stout, angular,
strong stems host a fan-shaped arrangement of
3, 5, or 7 leaflets that are woolly and whitish
underneath. Roselike flowers bloom May
through July and produce edible, juicy, black
berries July through September. The berries
can be used in jams and jellies.

HEIGHT: 3 to 12 feet.
RANGE: Throughout Midwest.

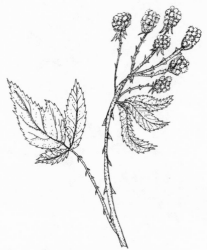

Black and Red Raspberry

Black and Red Raspberry　　　　WHITE
(Rubus occidentalis and *rubus idaeus)*

These two species found in woodland thickets
are nearly identical. Five leaflets are arranged
fanlike on purple, rambling vines with strong,
hooked prickles. White, roselike flowers
bloom April through July. Edible, black and
red berries are borne June through August.
They are used in jams, jellies, and pies.

HEIGHT:　Up to 12 feet.
RANGE:　Throughout Midwest.

Greenbrier

Greenbrier

GREEN

(Smilax rotundifolia)

This green-stemmed shrub of woods and thickets has a woody, stout, and thorny stalk with paired tendrils. Two-to-5-inch-long leaves are leathery, with conspicuous veins. Greenish flowers bloom April through June and bear blue-black berries September through winter.

HEIGHT: Depends on object upon which vine grows.

RANGE: Great Lakes area.

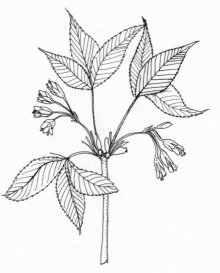

Bladdernut

Bladdernut WHITE
(Staphylea trifolia)

This shrub is found in fertile woodland soils, especially bottomland. Three or 5 paired leaflets are arranged featherlike on the leafstalk. They are fine toothed, elliptical, and 2 to 6 inches long. Clustered, drooping flowers bloom April through June. The seed is borne August through October in an unusual, inflated, papery case, 1 to 2 inches long.

HEIGHT: 5 to 15 feet.
RANGE: Minnesota, Ontario, Michigan.

American Yew

American Yew   UNSPECIFIED
(*Taxus canadensis*)

This shrubby conifer of moist woodlands
thrives in shades. One-inch needles are attached singly in flat sprays. The red, berrylike
fruit is ½ inch long and squat. The tree is often
used as an ornamental. The hard, close-
grained wood was used to make archery bows.

HEIGHT: 3 feet.
RANGE: Upper Midwest.

Common Highbush Blueberry

Common Highbush Blueberry   WHITE
(Vaccinium corymbosum)

Moist woods with acid soils are preferred by this member of the heath family. It has small, elliptical, short-stemmed leaves that are 1½ to 3½ inches long. Small, bell-like flowers bloom May through June. Edible, very tasty, blue or black berries containing many seeds are borne June through September. Greenish or reddish twigs are covered with tiny warts. This shrub is the basic stock from which many cultivated varieties of blueberries were developed.

HEIGHT: Up to 12 feet.
RANGE: Throughout Midwest.

Early Low Blueberry

Early Low Blueberry   WHITE
(*Vaccinium angustifolium*)

This low shrub of thickets and dry woods
prefers acid soils. Egg-shaped leaves, ½ to 2
inches long, may have a few bristle-tipped
teeth. They become leathery with age. Bell-
like flowers bloom April through June. Dark-
blue berries are covered with a white powder,
have many seeds, and are edible. The fruit is
borne June through September.

HEIGHT: 3 feet.
RANGE: Missouri, Michigan, Iowa, Ontario.

Smooth Blackhaw

Smooth Blackhaw   UNSPECIFIED
(*Viburnum prunifolium*)

This shrub is found in dry, rocky woods and in
hedgerows. Leaves are leathery, elliptical to
egg shaped, and 1 to 3 inches long. Flowers
bloom in small, stalkless clusters April through
May. Black, fleshy, and oblong berries containing one seed are borne September through
October. Short, stiff side twigs are attached to
main stalks.

HEIGHT: 6 to 15 feet.
RANGE: Illinois, Indiana, Missouri, Iowa,
          Michigan.

Cat Grape

Cat Grape   UNSPECIFIED
(*Vitis palmata*)

This vine is common to wet thickets, woods,
and some wetlands. Leaves are toothed, deeply
lobed, and 2 to 9 inches long. Flowers bloom
June through July, and clusters of black berries
are borne in October. Twigs usually are a
reddish color.

HEIGHT: Depends   on   height   of   object
          on which vine grows.
RANGE: Illinois, Indiana, Iowa.

4

The Wetlands

The wetlands of mid-North America are ecologically diverse, with a variety of plants and animals associated with them. Each wetland is intimately linked with the land surrounding it. Consequently, the effect of the land, as well as the distance from other wetland habitats, causes great variety in the kind of wetland plants found. Some of the most unique and beautiful flowers and trees found in the Midwest live in the wetland plant communities.

What is a wetland? Generally, it is any type of plant habitat characterized by a fairly saturated soil most of the year. Midwestern wetlands fit roughly six main categories: lakeshore, river or stream bank, pond, bog, marsh, and swamp. Each has a unique mixture of plants. The variety of plant types is caused by things that affect the wetland environment, such as climate, soil type, source of water, and amount of sunlight.

Despite the number of wetland types, the basic mixture of saturated soil, regional climate, and water creates fairly constant conditions. These conditions, in turn, have enabled many wetland plants to spread throughout the Midwest and elsewhere, giving rise to a rather consistent wetland plant community. Chances are that if you find yourself near a body of water in the Midwest, you are quite likely to find many of the same plant species you would find near another!

When exploring wetland plant communities, keep in mind the fact that several distinct plant zones, or plant subcommunities, exist. Sometimes these plant zones are seen quite easily, especially by a lakeshore or pond. As you walk from the higher, dry ground toward the water's edge, there are several distinct areas of vegetation.

In the outermost zone, bushy, young trees, such as alder, buttonbush, and willow, are rooted in the wet, spongy soil. In this area you can also find marsh marigold, grasses, horsetail, spearworts, and sedges. The next zone is wetter, with some standing water. Shallow water from the pond covers the lower stems and roots of the plants, but they are still basically land plants in character. Bulrushes, cattails, and the wild blue flag iris are common.

Unless you are wearing sneakers or rubber boots, you may not be able to explore the next zone. It is an area of what are called emergent plants—plants rooted up to a foot or more beneath the surface of the pond.

Sphagnum moss, rushes, and cattails are found on the perimeter of this zone, slowly advancing and filling the pond. Beyond them, swamp loosestrife (water willow) is pushing out into deeper water, grasping the bottom with reddish roots. In one season, given the right conditions, this plant may grow three feet into the pond. In the same area, tussock sedges flourish, capturing sediment at the base of their closely growing stalks.

Farther out in the pond are pickerelweeds, arrowheads, and spike rushes, with just a few leaves poking above the surface. Lilies grow beside them and extend even farther out, rooted in water as deep as six feet or more. Beyond this last, floating leaf zone, submerged plants grow in abundance as long as there is enough daily sunlight to support their growth. Plants of the submergent varieties have not been included in this book because they are difficult to observe and identify.

Although the wetland is a relatively stable environment, it is slowly, continuously changing. The zones of the lake or pond are a good example of the slow and steady changes that occur, and they are fairly easy to see as described.

What do the various zones and types of plants imply? Can you see how the plants might slowly move toward the center of the pond?

The pioneer plants of submergents and emergents grow each season and die in the fall. The pond's soil is enriched as these plants decay. Other plants requiring this richer soil then take root. Their sturdier stalks hold more sediment, and they, in turn, die and decay. Over a period of many years the sediment builds up, giving wetland trees and shrubs a place to root and grow. The pond or lake gradually becomes shallower and smaller. Eventually, it becomes a bog or marsh and then, perhaps, a prairie meadow.

Become familiar with a particular pond or lake to which you have ready access. Usually over a period of years, but sometimes over a single summer, you can observe changes in the shoreline created by this dynamic process, which biologists call plant succession. Determine the depth of the pond and its average temperature throughout the year. Try to determine the number of hours of summer sunlight the pond receives. All these things will effect the kind of wetland plant community you will find.

Flowers

Grassy Arrowhead

Grassy Arrowhead   WHITE
(Sagittaria graminea)

Grassy-leaved Arrowhead

The grassy or lance-shaped leaves do not have the characteristic shape of most arrowheads. However, the blossoms are similar, arranged in threes on a freestanding stalk. The tiny, white flower is composed of 3 white petals. Blooms July to October.

HEIGHT: 1 to 3 feet.
RANGE: Throughout Midwest.

Broad-leaved Arrowhead

Broad-leaved Arrowhead   WHITE
(Sagittaria Latifolia)

Duck Potato

This arrowhead gets its name from the obvious shape of the unusual, arrowhead-shaped leaves. There is considerable differentiation in the leaf proportions, sometimes within the same species. The best way to identify the common broad-leaved arrowhead is by the flower stalk, with sets of 3 white flowers, each of which consists of 3 petals. Blooms July to October.

HEIGHT: 1 to 6 feet.
RANGE: Throughout Midwest.

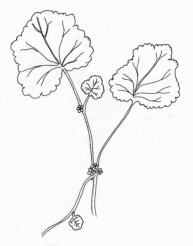

Water Pennywort

Water Pennywort   WHITE
(Hydrocotyle americana)

This creeping member of the parsley family
has 1 to 5 tiny flowers and roundish leaves
with a shallowly scalloped edge.

HEIGHT: 1 foot.
RANGE: Ontario and northern edge of U. S.

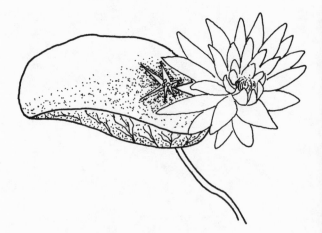

Scented Pond Lily

Scented Pond Lily   WHITE
Fragrant Water Lily
(Nymphaea odorata)

This spectacular, white water lily is found in standing bodies of water and sluggish streams. The leaf is a notched, round-bladed lily pad that floats on the water's surface. It has a slightly veined, purplish underside. The 3-to-5-inch blossom has many tapering petals that gradually become smaller toward the center and is characterized by a strong, pleasant fragrance. Blooms June to October.

HEIGHT: 1 to 6 feet (submerged).
RANGE: Throughout Midwest.

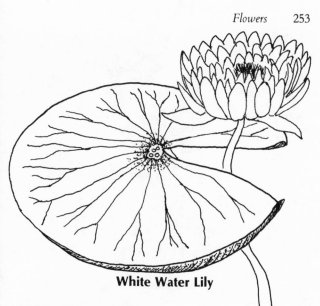

White Water Lily

White Water Lily

WHITE

Tuberous Water Lily

(Nymphaea tuberosa)

This 3-to-5-inch flower has numerous, broadly rounded, white petals that become smaller toward the center. Although similar in appearance to the scented pond lily, it lacks a strong fragrance. The floating leaf is notched and round, with light veining on top and a light green underside.

HEIGHT: 1 to 6 feet (submerged).
RANGE: Throughout Midwest.

Water Hemlock

Water Hemlock   WHITE
Spotted Cowbane
(*Cicuta maculata*)

This member of the parsley family is found in
wet soils of swamp, marsh, or meadow.
Coarsely toothed leaves occur in sets of 2 or 3
and are often reddish. They are attached to a
smooth, stout stem streaked with purple. Very
poisonous flowers bloom June through September. Other parts also are poisonous. It is
similar to the smaller bulblet water hemlock
(*Cicuta bulbifera*), also poisonous.

HEIGHT: 3 to 6 feet.
RANGE: Missouri, Iowa, Illinois.

Cuckooflower

Cuckooflower   WHITE/PINK
(*Cardamine pratensis*)

This plant is found in swamps and wet woodlands. Leaves near the base are roundish or
oval, with upper stem leaves slender. Clusters
of small, 4-petaled flowers bloom April
through June at the top of the stem.

HEIGHT: 2 feet.
RANGE: Common in Ontario, Minnesota, Illi-
          nois, Indiana.

Broad-leaved Water Plantain

Broad-leaved Water Plantain   WHITE
(Alisma plantago-aquatica)

This plant grows in moist soil, mud, or shallow water. Leaves are oblong, with a heart-shaped or rounded base. Three-petaled flowers grow on bushy stalks.

HEIGHT: 3 to 36 inches.
RANGE: Common throughout Midwest.

Swamp Rose Mallow

Swamp Rose Mallow　　　　　WHITE/PINK
Marsh Hibiscus
(*Hibiscus palustris*)

Leaves are rough edged and variable in shape.
Large, white-to-pink, cone-shaped flowers are
unmistakable, measuring 4 to 7 inches across.
Blooms August through September.

HEIGHT:　2 to 7 feet.
RANGE　Throughout most of the Midwest.

Beak Rush

Beak Rush   WHITE
White Beaked Rush
(*Rhynchospora alba*)

The 3-sided, pale green stem is sometimes very
tall. A plain, white flower produces a beak-
shaped seed.

HEIGHT: 6 to 20 inches.
RANGE: Southern Midwest.

Watercress

Watercress   WHITE
(*Nasturtium officinale*)

This smooth plant with traveling stems that
float, or creep, is found in or by running
water, particularly springs. It has 3 to 9 oval
leaflets with rounded lobes. Flowers bloom in
small clusters April through June. It is often
used for making delicious salads.

HEIGHT: 4 to 10 inches.
RANGE: Throughout Midwest.

Bullhead Lily
(Nuphar variegatum)
Yellow Water Lily
(Nuphar advena)
Small Pond Lily
(Nuphar microphyllum)

YELLOW

These three lilies are visually identical, with only subtle differentiations between species. They are all found in standing or sluggish bodies of water. They are characterized by 1-to-2-inch, sulfur-colored, ball-shaped flowers made up of 5 or more cupped petals that conceal a disklike stigma in the center. Leaves are fleshy and oval shaped with a narrow notch. The leaf and blossom of the yellow water lily are usually found erect above the water, and those of the other two species are always found floating. The small pond lily has a flower 1 inch or less in diameter. Blooms June to October.

HEIGHT: 2 to 6 feet.

RANGE: Bullhead lily—Northern Illinois, Indiana, Iowa, and north through Ontario.

Yellow water lily—Southern Wisconsin and Michigan and south.

Small pond lily—Minnesota, Wisconsin, Michigan, and north through Ontario.

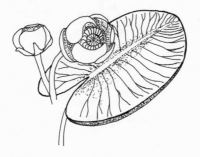

Bullhead Lily, Yellow Water Lily, and Small Pond Lily

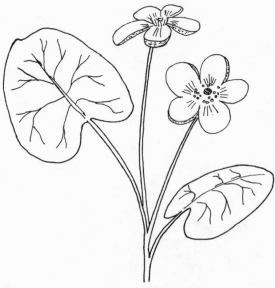

Marsh Marigold

Marsh Marigold   YELLOW
Cowslip
(*Caltha palustris*)

This plant is found in swamps and along
streams. Glossy and roundish or kidney-shaped
leaves grow on a thick, succulent, hollow
stem. Flowers are actually made up of 5 to 9
deep yellow sepals that look like petals.
Blooms April through June.

HEIGHT: 8 to 24 inches.
RANGE: Common throughout Midwest.

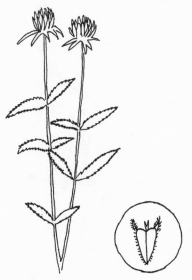

Swamp Beggar-ticks

Swamp Beggar-ticks   YELLOW
(*Bidens connata*)

This small flower grows singly or in clusters
with a dark center. Large, pointed leaves
growing from the stalk are lance shaped and
toothed. The flat seed has 2 or 4 barbs. Blooms
August through October.

HEIGHT: 3 to 6 inches.
RANGE: Throughout Midwest.

Sweet Flag

Sweet Flag   YELLOW
(*Acorus calamus*)

A narrow, flat, leaflike stem bears a cigar-shaped cone of flowers, 1 to 3 inches long, that juts out at an angle partway up the stem. Leaves are tall and narrow, resembling the stem. Blooms May through August.

HEIGHT: 1 to 3 feet.
RANGE: Throughout Midwest.

Water Star Grass

Water Star Grass   YELLOW
(Heteranthera dubia)

Found from shallow to deep water, this
member of the pickerelweed family often
becomes stranded on mudbanks. Leaves are
grasslike and flaccid, 5 to 10 inches long, and
usually submerged. The small, pale yellow
flower blooms June to September.

HEIGHT: ½ to 5 feet (submerged).
RANGE: Illinois, Minnesota, Wisconsin, On-
          tario.

Floating Water Primrose

Floating Water Primrose   YELLOW
Creeping Primrose Willow
(*Jussiaea repens*)

A creeping or floating root stem supports this plant's large, yellow flowers and oblong, untoothed leaves. Rose-colored stems are a distinguishing characteristic. The 4-to-6-petaled flower blooms June through August.

HEIGHT: Up to 10 feet.
RANGE: Southeastern   Midwest   (southern Missouri, Illinois, Indiana).

Floating Arum

Floating Arum   YELLOW
Golden Club
(*Orontium aquaticum*)

The distinctive, wide, elliptical leaves of this
plant are usually found floating in the shallow
water of swamps or ponds. A club-shaped tip
covered with tiny, yellow flowers blooms on
the stalk April through June.

HEIGHT: 2 feet.
RANGE: Throughout Midwest.

Golden Ragwort

Golden Ragwort   YELLOW
(Senecio aureus)

This meadow flower has finely cut leaves attached to its stem, while those at the base are long stemmed, heart shaped, and often reddish underneath. The flower blooms May through July in flat-topped clusters with sparse rays in each flower.

HEIGHT: 1 to 3 feet.
RANGE: Throughout Midwest.

Bog Goldenrod

Bog Goldenrod   YELLOW
(Solidago uliginosa)

This smooth-stemmed plant of swamps and bogs has distinctive, plumelike, yellow flowers. Lancelike leaves with shallow teeth are up to 1 foot long on the lower stalk.

HEIGHT: 2 to 5 feet.
RANGE: Wisconsin, Minnesota, Ontario.

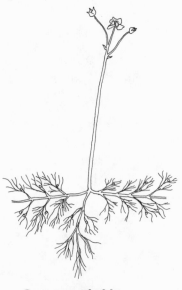

Common Bladderwort

Common Bladderwort   YELLOW
(Utricularia vulgaris)

An aquatic, free-floating plant, it has small air bladders for catching insects on leaves or branches. Thin, filamentlike leaves submerged in shallow water or mud float horizontally with few or no aerial leaves. The bright yellow flower, reminiscent of a snapdragon, blooms May through August.

HEIGHT: Up to 1 foot.
RANGE: Common throughout Midwest.

Adder's-tongue

Adder's-tongue   YELLOW
(Ophioglossum vulgatum)

This plant can be found in wet soils of marshes
and lakeshores. It has a single, spoon-shaped
leaf with a spore-bearing spike growing out of
its center. Blooms May through August.

HEIGHT: 5 to 15 inches.
RANGE: Upper Midwest.

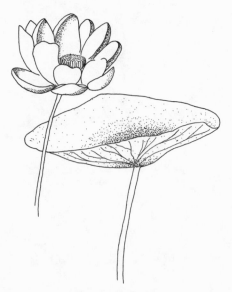

Common Lotus

Common Lotus   YELLOW
(*Nelumbo lutea*)

This member of the water-lily family prefers
sluggish rivers and ponds. The leaf is somewhat varied but generally bowl shaped, about
2 feet long, and often grows above the water's
surface. The flower is up to 10 inches in
diameter. Seeds are borne symmetrically in a
distinctive, round head.

HEIGHT: 2 to 6 feet.
RANGE: Throughout Midwest.

Northern Willow Herb

Northern Willow Herb PINK
(Epilobium glandulosum)

This plant gets its name from the narrow, willowlike leaves that are attached directly to the stem. A 4-petaled flower blooms July through September. Seedpods have seeds with whitish hairs.

HEIGHT: 1 to 3 feet.
RANGE: Upper Midwest.

Swamp Thistle

Swamp Thistle
(Cirsium muticum)

RED/PURPLE

This plant grows in swamps or wet prairie thickets and favors alkaline soils. It has single or clustered flowers on long stalks and toothed, multilobed leaves. Blooms July through September.

HEIGHT: 2 to 10 feet.
RANGE: Illinois.

Swamp Milkweed

Swamp Milkweed
(Asclepias incarnata)

DULL PINK

This plant has broad, flat flower masses made up of tiny, cuplike flowers. Narrow, lance-shaped leaves grow from a sometimes short, sometimes bushy stalk characterized by a thick, milky white juice if broken. Blooms June through September.

HEIGHT: 2 to 4 feet.
RANGE: Very common throughout Midwest.

Narrow-leafed Water Plantain

Narrow-leafed Water Plantain   ROSE
(Alisma geyeri)   OR WHITE

This plant grows in mud or shallow water. It has spear-shaped leaves and small, 3-petaled flowers on bushy stalks. Although terrestrial leaves are only 4 to 6 inches long, those submerged or partially submerged can attain a length of 3 feet or more. Blooms July through September.

HEIGHT: Up to 2 feet.
RANGE: Throughout Midwest but less common in extreme southern portions.

Round-leaved Sundew

Round-leaved Sundew   PINK/WHITE
(*Drosera rotundifolia*)

This unusual plant, which kills insects for
nourishment, is common in acidic or peaty bog
environments. A set of small, round leaves
grows on slender stalks from the base of the
flower stem. Each leaf is covered with reddish
hairs that exude a sticky juice that looks like
dewdrops. Insects attracted to the leaf stick to
the attractive "dew," which dissolves them.
The leaf then absorbs the insects' nutrients. A
small, cluster of delicate flowers blooms at the
tip of a slender stem that rises from the base of
the leafstalk. Blooms June through August.

HEIGHT: 1 foot.
RANGE: Throughout Midwest.

Marsh St.-John's-Wort

Marsh St.-John's-Wort   PINK
(*Hypericum virginicum*)

This habitant of bogs and swamps has 1-to-3-inch oval leaves that embrace the stem in pairs. The 5-petaled flower is pink, not the characteristic yellow of other St.-John's-worts.

HEIGHT: 1 to 2 feet.
RANGE: Great Lakes area.

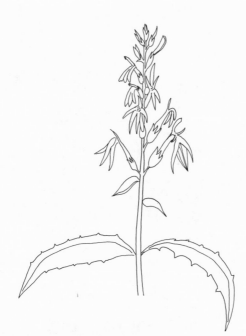

Cardinal Flower

Cardinal Flower   RED
(*Lobelia cardinalis*)

This startling, red flower grows in a slender
spike. Leaves are toothed, lance shaped, and
tapering to a short stalk. Blooms July through
August.

HEIGHT: 5 feet.
RANGE: Upper Midwest.

Common Three-square

Common Three-square   RED/BROWN
(Scirpus americanus)

The leaves of this rush are long, narrow
blades, usually 1 to 3 per stem. The stem, in
turn, has a sharp, 3-sided stem with a red
brown spiked cluster of tiny flowers at the
top. The stem was used by chairmakers to
weave seats.

HEIGHT: 3 to 6 feet.
RANGE: Throughout Midwest.

Purple Loosestrife

Purple Loosestrife   RED/PURPLE
(*Lythrum salicaria*)

This shrublike plant roots in wet soils of
shorelines. Lance-shaped leaves are arranged
on the stem either opposite or in sets of three.
A 4-to-6-petaled flower blooms in a spikelike
cluster June through August.

HEIGHT: 3 to 6 feet.
RANGE: Throughout Midwest.

False Loosestrife

False Loosestrife
RED/GREEN
(*Ludwigia palustris*)

This plant of shorelines and shallow waters forms floating tangles of reddish stems. Glossy, red-veined leaves are attached in pairs. A 4-parted flower grows at the base of the leaves.

HEIGHT: 4 to 6 inches.
RANGE: Throughout Midwest.

Water Smartweed

Water Smartweed   RED
(Polygonum amphibium)

Adapting readily to environmental changes,
this "smart" plant varies from aquatic forms
with floating leaves to a hairy, terrestrial
form. The easiest way to identify the plant is
by its stubby, red flower clusters, which
bloom June through September.

HEIGHT: 2 to 4 feet.
RANGE: Throughout Midwest.

Swamp Smartweed

Swamp Smartweed   PINK/SCARLET
(*Polygonum coccineum*)

Extremely variable in form, this plant ranges
from floating to terrestrial habitats. It can be
recognized because of a sheath-covered, knot-
like swelling on the stem at each leaf joint.
Tiny flowers bloom at the stalk tip in a tight,
spikelike cluster July through September.

HEIGHT: 2 to 4 feet.
RANGE: Throughout Midwest.

Pitcher Plant

Pitcher Plant   RED
(Sarracenia purpurea)

This unmistakable plant has reddish, urn-
shaped leaves filled with a watery liquid that
digests insects that fall into it. The pendulous,
globe-shaped flower hangs bell-like on a separate stalk. Blooms May through July.

HEIGHT: Up to 2 feet.
RANGE: Throughout Midwest.

Water Lobelia

Water Lobelia   VIOLET
(Lobelia dortmanna)

This unusual plant has a stem that grows above the waterline and bears several pretty flowers, while a tuft of leaves grows around its submerged base. Leaves are narrow and ern Ontario.

HEIGHT: 8 to 18 inches.
RANGE: Throughout Midwest except north-
           ern Ontario.

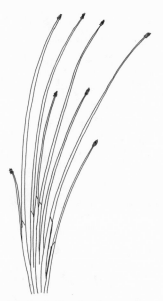

Blunt Spike Rush

Blunt Spike Rush

BROWN

(Elocharis obtusa)

This marshland rush grows in distinct clumps.
It has a single brown spike of flowers growing
at the top.

HEIGHT: 3 to 12 inches.
RANGE: Throughout Midwest.

Marsh Bellflower

Marsh Bellflower   VIOLET/BLUE
(*Campanula aparinoides*)

This delicate flower is distinctly bell-like, both in shape and the way it hangs on its stalk. It has narrow leaves with hairlike bristles. Blooms June through August.

HEIGHT: 1 foot.
RANGE: Common throughout Midwest except Missouri.

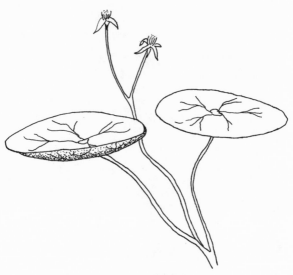

Water Shield

Water Shield   DULL PURPLE
(Brassenia schreberi)

Along with other members of the water-lily
family, it grows in ponds or slow streams. A
small, 2-or-3-inch leaf floats at the end of a
long, slimy submerged stem. The stem and leaf
underside have a gelatinlike coating. Flowers
are very small, about ¾ of an inch long, with 3
or 4 petals. They bloom June through September.

HEIGHT: Variable.
RANGE: Throughout Midwest.

Larger Blue Flag

Larger Blue Flag
(*Iris versicolor*)

BLUE

This beauty of the wetlands is a violet-to-blue native iris. Graceful, sword-shaped leaves are crowned by the flower, with its 2-inch, down-curved, veined sepals. Petals flip upward around the stamen, creating an unusually showy wild flower. Blooms June and July.

HEIGHT: 2 to 3 feet.
RANGE: Minnesota, Wisconsin, Michigan, Ontario.

Pickerelweed

Pickerelweed   BLUE
(*Pontederia cordata*)

This common plant of shallow water has a
large leaf shaped like an arrowhead and a stalk
crowned by a spike of several small flowers
about 1 inch across. Blooms June through October.

HEIGHT: 1 to 4 feet.
RANGE: Lower Ontario southward.

Water Avens

Water Avens   PURPLE/YELLOW
Purple Avens
(*Geum rivale*)

This flower blooms May to August in bogs, meadows, and similar wet places. Nodding, globular flowers usually occur in sets of 3 and hang from a curved stalk.

HEIGHT: 1 to 4 feet.
RANGE: Illinois, Wisconsin, Minnesota.

Wild Mint

Wild Mint   VIOLET/WHITE
(Mentha arvensis)

Although several species of mint are difficult
to distinguish, they all have a distinct mintlike
fragrance. Because of this, large beds of wild
mint can sometimes be detected downwind.
Paired, stalkless leaves are oval in shape with a
toothed edge. Tiny, bell-shaped flowers bloom
July through September at the point where the
leaf attaches to the stem.

HEIGHT: ½ to 2 feet.
RANGE: Throughout Midwest.

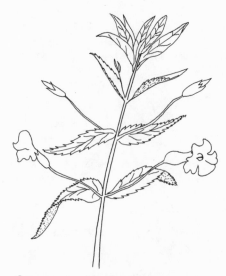

Square-stemmed Monkey Flower

Square-stemmed Monkey Flower   VIOLET
(*Mimulus ringens*)

The leaves of this plant are paired and attached directly to the stem. The flower has 5 lobed petals. The 2 upper lobes are erect, and the 3 lower are spread. The mouth of the flower may be partly closed by a pair of yellow ridges. Flowers bloom June through September on long stalks at the junction of leaf and stem.

HEIGHT: 1 to 3 feet.
RANGE: Throughout Midwest.

Arrow Arum

Arrow Arum
GREEN
(*Peltandra virginica*)

This plant favors shallow waters. Leaves have a distinctive triangular or arrowhead shape. The flower is very small and crowded, growing in a leafy covering. Blooms May through July. Berries are borne in a globular head and turn brown at maturity.

HEIGHT: 1 to 1½ feet.
RANGE: Throughout Midwest.

Bur Reed and Giant Bur Reed GREEN/BROWN
(Sparganium eurycarpum)

So many species of bur reed are found that
they are difficult to identify. Related to cattails, these two species are frequently the
dominant plants on ponds or lakeshores. They
have long, slender stalks and leaves up to 1
inch wide, with small, simple flowers growing
separately. Seeds are borne in dense clusters,
on separate stalks.

HEIGHT: Up to 4 feet.
RANGE: About 10 species in North America,
with most occurring in Midwest and
North.

Bur Reed and Giant Bur Reed

Common Cattail
(*Typha latifolia*)
Narrow-leaved Cattail
(*Typha angustifolia*)

BROWN

The most common of midwestern wetland plants, the cattail borders on being a pest. It grows with a vengeance, springing up in clusters wherever it finds enough moisture to root. Cattails are aggressive colonizers of shallow waters with mud bottoms. They capture sediment and speed the process of filling. Flowers are very simple and small, condensed into long, distinctive, brown cylinders. Leaves are erect and bladelike. Young shoots are edible, raw or cooked, as are the young flower shoots. The common cattail is larger, with leaves up to 2 inches wide, the narrow-leaved cattail having slim leaves only about ¼ inch wide. The latter is also shorter and can be distinguished by the gap between flower cylinder and the fluffy staminate material higher on the stem.

HEIGHT:　Common cattail—3 to 7 feet.
　　　　　Narrow-leaved cattail—4 to 5 feet.
RANGE:　Common cattail—Throughout Midwest.
　　　　　Narrow-leaved cattail—Lower Midwest.

Narrow-leaved Cattail

Common Cattail

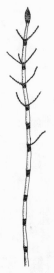

Swamp Horsetail

Swamp Horsetail
(Equisetum fluviatile)

NO FLOWER

This primitive is one of the oldest living land plants. The jointed main stem looks like bamboo and actually pulls apart (children enjoy playing with the sections). Thin, needlelike leaves radiate from the stem joints. A small cone at the top of the stalk sheds pollen. The plant grows in shallow water and mudbanks May until the first freeze.

HEIGHT: 2 to 5 feet.
RANGE: Throughout Midwest.

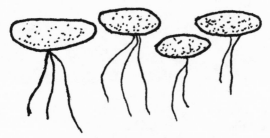

Giant Duckweed

Giant Duckweed
(Spirodela polyrhiza)

This plant is very small and not differentiated into stems and leaves. Among the smallest known flowering plants in the world, the individual plants are only 3 to 10 millimeters long. They are oval shaped, and are green above, with purplish undersides. They float in clusters on still water surfaces during summer.

HEIGHT: Stemless.
RANGE: Illinois.

Trees

Red Maple

Red Maple
(*Acer rubrum*)

This tree has a high, elongated crown and often exceeds 2 feet in diameter. Leaves have 3 to 5 lobes on a long, slender, reddish leafstalk. Two single-winged seeds attached at their stems drop between May and July. The bark is smooth on young trees and new growth.

HEIGHT: 80 feet.
RANGE: Throughout Midwest.

River Birch (Red Birch)

River Birch
(Red Birch)
(Betula nigra)

With an irregular crown and slightly drooping, slender branches, this tree is similar to the
paper birch. The curled, shredded texture of
the reddish brown bark makes the tree easily
recognizable. A simple, oval-shaped leaf, 3
inches long, with a coarsely double-toothed
edge is characterized by a woody, brittle
leafstalk. The tree produces a thick, 1½ inch,
cylindrical-shaped package of tiny nutlets,
each with a 3-lobed wing.

HEIGHT: Up to 70 feet at maturity.
RANGE: Central Illinois, Missouri, and Indi-
          ana southward.

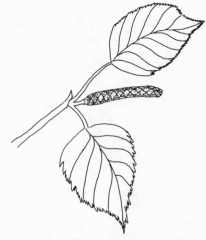

Paper Birch

Paper Birch
(Betula payrifera)

A versatile tree, it is common to both northern forests and wetlands. Oval-shaped leaves,
3 inches long, have a coarse, saw-toothed
edge. A drooping, cylindrical catkin bears
minute seeds attached to a 3-lobed membrane,
or wing. The stark, white bark with black
highlights contrasts strikingly with the evergreen forest. It splits into paperlike layers at
maturity.

HEIGHT: 70 feet.
RANGE: Upper Midwest.

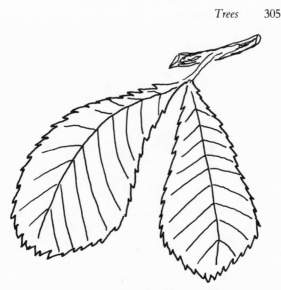

Swamp Birch

Swamp Birch
(Betula pumila)

This tree grows with a low, bushy profile, sometimes branched to the ground. Egg-shaped, toothed leaves, ½ to 4 inches long, are green with almost white undersides. The bark is characteristically shaggy in patches.

HEIGHT: 2 to 12 feet.
RANGE: Indiana, Michigan, Ontario.

Swamp Ash

Swamp Ash
(Black Ash)
(Fraxinus nigra)

This tree is most common in floodplains and swamps. Seven to 11 toothed leaves are attached directly to a single stem and bloom April to May. Seeds, blunt at both ends, may be found June through September. Mature trees have a scalelike bark that readily flakes off when scraped.

HEIGHT: 40 to 80 feet.
RANGE: Throughout Upper Midwest.

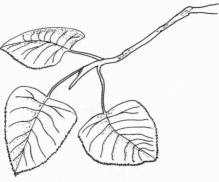

Common Cottonwood

Common Cottonwood
(Populus deltoides)

This monarch of midwestern stream banks and bottomlands roots deeply in rich soils and grows rapidly to tremendous proportions, up to 8 feet or more in diameter. Its spreading crown is broadly rounded, with some drooping branches. Coarsely toothed leaves are triangular, tapering to a point and having a flat base. An elliptical, ¼ inch, greenish brown capsule contains numerous seeds with white cottony hairs attached. The bark is smooth and gray when young but becomes furrowed at maturity.

HEIGHT: 80 to 100 feet at maturity.
RANGE: Throughout Midwest.

Swamp Oak

Swamp Oak
(*Quercus bicolor*)

As its name implies, this oak prefers the semi-saturated soils of swamp and wet bottomland. Leaves are rounded and toothed with a wavy edge. Their undersides are usually white and hairy. The acorn has distinctively long stalks, ranging from 1 to 2½ inches in length.

HEIGHT: 60 to 70 feet at maturity.
RANGE: Lower Ontario southward.

Black Willow

Black Willow
(Salix nigra)

Almost as common to wetlands as cattails, this tree can grow from a brushy young pioneer at water's edge to a large, spreading tree with black limbs and trunk at maturity. This tree plays an important role in stabilizing and holding soil with its strong roots. Leaves are 3 to 6 inches long and narrow; green on both sides and attached to long, somewhat drooping branches. Although weak, wood is used for boxes and crates. It is extremely light and used for artificial limbs.

HEIGHT: 3 to 40 feet.
RANGE: Throughout Midwest.

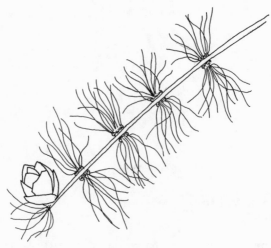

Tamarack

Tamarack
(Larix laricina)

This tree is a beautiful conifer of northern bogs and swamps. The leaves are needles up to 1 inch long that grow in numerous clusters along the branches. They are shed in the autumn. A chestnut brown, oblong cone, ½ to an inch long, is borne.

HEIGHT: 50 to 60 feet.
RANGE: Upper Midwest.

Shrubs

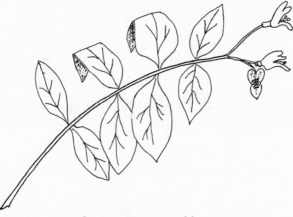

Swamp Honeysuckle

Swamp Honeysuckle
YELLOW
(Lonicera oblongifolia)

This inhabitant of northern bogs and white cedar swamps has oblong or egg-shaped leaves that are 1 to 3½ inches long and more or less hairless. Yellowish, sticky, and hairy flowers bloom May through June. They produce orange or red berries July and August.

HEIGHT: Up to 5 feet.
RANGE: Michigan, Minnesota.

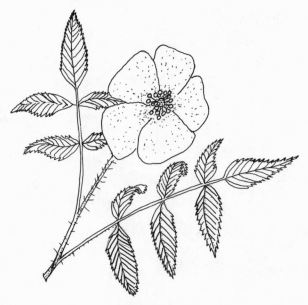

Swamp Rose

Swamp Rose
(Rosa palustris)

PINK

A bushy plant of wet ground, this delicate wild rose has a simple flower with 5 petals and finely toothed tapering leaves paired on the twig.

HEIGHT:　3 feet.
RANGE:　Lower Ontario extending south.

Swamp Loosestrife

Swamp Loosestrife   PURPLE OR RED
(Decodon verticillatus)

This woody, long-stemmed pioneer is con-
stantly pushing out to populate the shores of
ponds and lakes. Narrow, lance-shaped leaves,
2 to 5 inches long, resemble willow leaves.
They grow on short stalks in pairs or in threes.
A showy, red-to-purple flower, bell shaped
with 5 petals, blooms July through August.

HEIGHT: 2 to 7 feet.
RANGE: Eastern Midwest and Minnesota.

Poison Sumac

Poison Sumac
GREEN

(Rhus vernix)

This shrub grows in partly wooded lowlands and swamps. Smooth-edged, 6-to-12-inch leaflets grow 7 to 13 on a leaf stem. They turn a distinctive red or yellow in autumn. Small, greenish flowers bloom in clusters May through July. White or grayish berries appear in August and may stay attached until spring. Every part of this plant is poisonous, even to the touch.

HEIGHT: 6 to 12 feet.
RANGE: Lower Ontario southward.

Index